SINISTER DEXTER

GUNSHARK VACATION

SINISTER DEXTER CREATED BY

DAN ABNETT

DAVID MILLGATE

2000 AD

DC COMICS

SINISTER DEXTER

Script: Dan Abnett

Art: David Millgate

Colors: Junior Tomlin

Letters: Ellie de Ville

Originally published in *2000 AD* Winter Special 1995

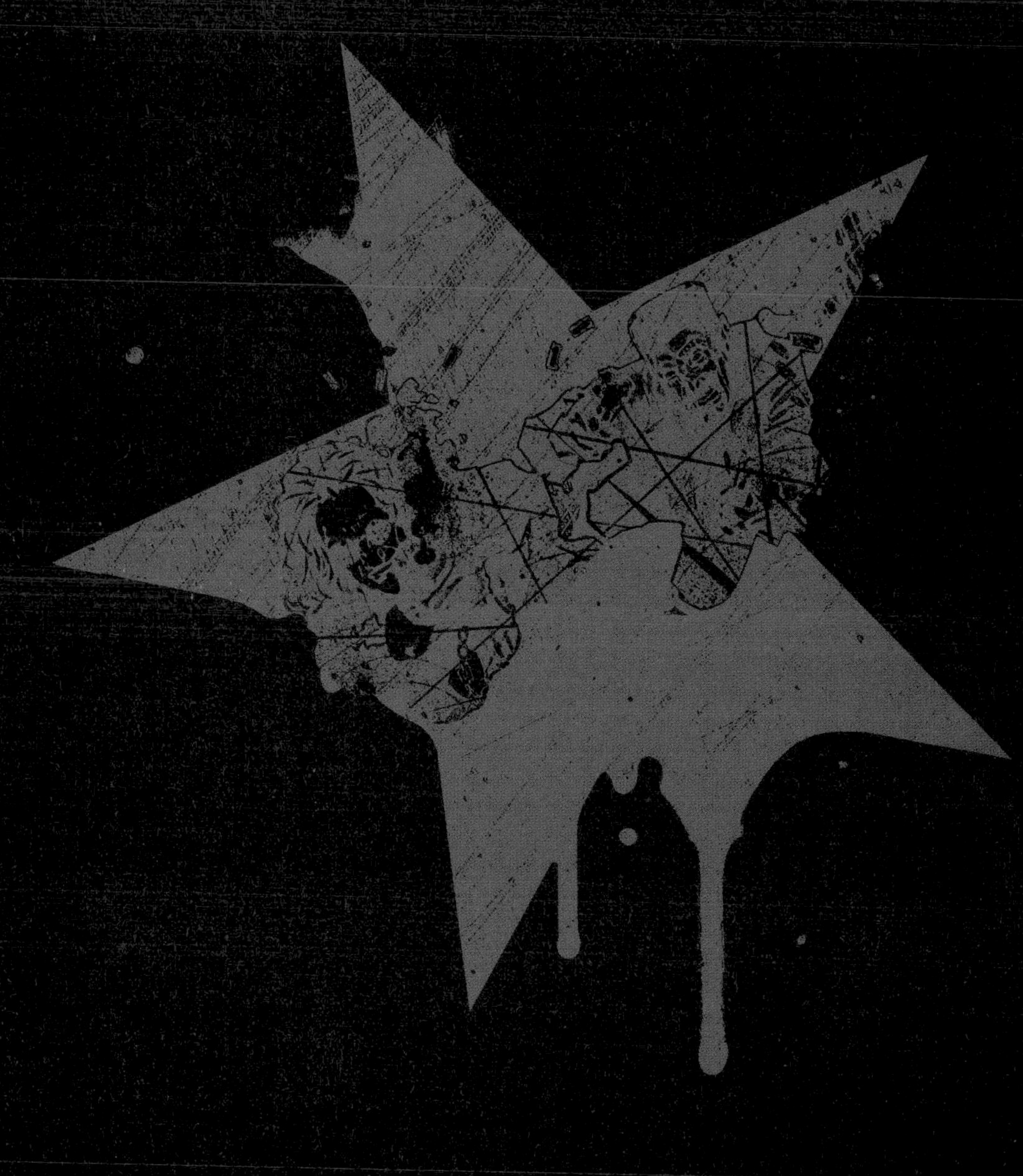

SINISTER DEXTER

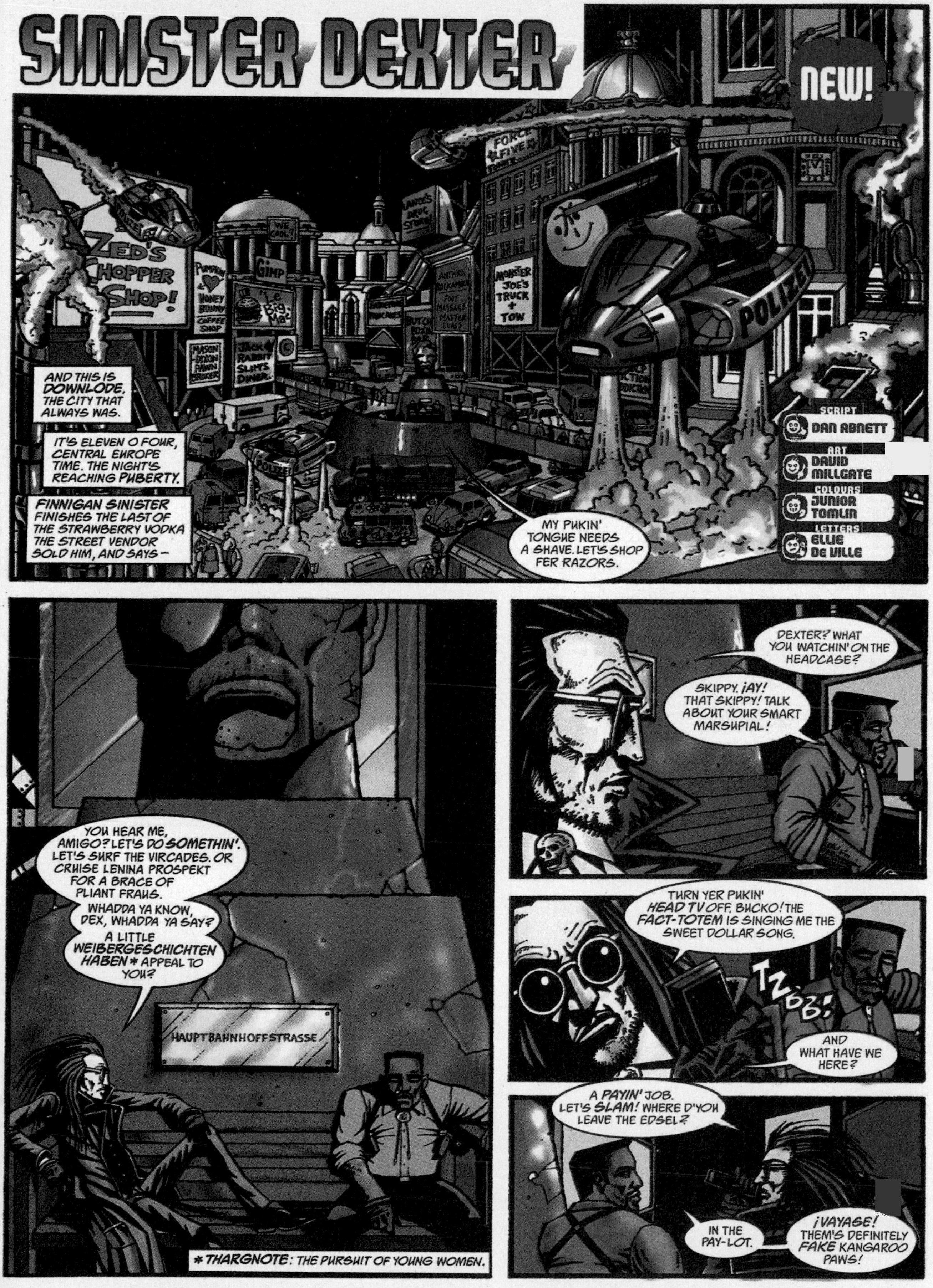

SINISTER DEXTER

NEW!

AND THIS IS **DOWNLODE**, THE CITY THAT ALWAYS WAS.

IT'S ELEVEN O FOUR, CENTRAL EUROPE TIME. THE NIGHT'S REACHING **PUBERTY**.

FINNIGAN SINISTER FINISHES THE LAST OF THE STRAWBERRY VODKA THE STREET VENDOR SOLD HIM, AND SAYS –

MY PUKIN' TONGUE NEEDS A SHAVE. LET'S SHOP FER RAZORS.

SCRIPT DAN ABNETT

ART DAVID MILLGATE

COLOURS JUNIOR TOMLIN

LETTERS ELLIE DE VILLE

YOU HEAR ME, AMIGO? LET'S DO SOMETHIN'. LET'S SURF THE VIRCADES. OR CRUISE LENINA PROSPEKT FOR A BRACE OF PLIANT FRAUS.
WHADDA YA KNOW, DEX, WHADDA YA SAY?
A LITTLE WEIBERGESCHICHTEN HABEN* APPEAL TO YOU?
HAUPTBAHNHOFFSTRASSE
*THARGNOTE: THE PURSUIT OF YOUNG WOMEN.

DEXTER? WHAT YOU WATCHIN' ON THE HEADCASE?
SKIPPY. ¡AY! THAT SKIPPY! TALK ABOUT YOUR SMART MARSUPIAL!

TURN YER PUKIN' HEAD TV OFF, BUCKO! THE FACT-TOTEM IS SINGING ME THE SWEET DOLLAR SONG.
TZBB!
AND WHAT HAVE WE HERE?

A PAYIN' JOB. LET'S SLAM! WHERE D'YOU LEAVE THE EDSEL?
IN THE PAY-LOT.
¡VAYASE! THEM'S DEFINITELY FAKE KANGAROO PAWS!

WHO'S THE STIFF?
SOME MOOK CALLED **GNOME**. TOTEM SAID HE'S A VIRTUAL VANDAL. *TCHA!* GUY'S GOTTA HAVE A HOBBY, I SUPPOSE.

HANG A LEFT AT THE BAUSTELLE. WE NEED TO HIT THE CZAR'S **BLACK MARKET** AND BUY US SOME **SMARTS**.
WE SHOULD TRY **FLOPPY** FIRST.
THIS THEY THEN *DO*, MY MAN!

PRIVYET, BOYS! LONK TIME!
PRIVYET **YOURSELF**, VANYA! LOOKING GOOD, MATE!
YOU BOYS BUYINK OR SELLINK TONIGHT? WE GOT MARLBORO RED, TAIWANESE TEQUILA, SOME **GROOVEY** BARE NAKIT LADEEZ!

MAYBE LATER, VANYA. WE'RE LOOKING FOR FLOPPY.
OVER BY THE FENCE. YOU WONT I SHOOD WOTCH THE EDSEL WHALL YOR GONE?
SPASIBA. ANY STRIFE FROM THE HEAT TONIGHT?

NYET! THEY **KNOW** NOT TO NOSE AROUNT.
WHOOO-HOO! **NICE** KILLWARE, TOVARISCH!
GIVE MY BEST TO THE CZAR.
YOU HAVE MY **DEEPEST** SYMPATHY.
I LOVE THIS PLACE, DEX! THIS IS WHY GOD MADE THE PAPER RUBLE. I CAN **SMELL** THE MONEY. **HARD** MONEY. FOLDING GREEN. NONE OF THAT NETFUND PUKE.
¡AY! SKIPPY IS OVER!

FINNIGAN! RAMONE! WHAT'S THE GOOD WORD?
CRUD
CON
EVISCERATE IS A PERSONAL FAVOURITE. HOW'S IT HANGING, FLOPPY?
THIRTY DEGREES TO WINDWARD. HOPE YOU HAVEN'T COME FOR A REFUND.

AS IF. DEX JUST LURVES THE SONY HEADCASE YOU SOLD HIM. SIXTY DOLLARS, NO QUESTIONS. HAVEN'T HAD A STRAIGHT CONVERSATION WITH HIM SINCE.
SONY
SHUSH! DESI JUST GOT HOME AND LUCY IS TRYING TO HIDE THE ADULT APPLIANCES...

REMAKES. BLIGHT OF THE WESTERN WORLD.
SONY
SO WHAT DO YOU WANT?
HOOOOO, LUUCY!

LOOKING FOR A NET PIRATE BY THE NAME OF GNOME. ANY TIPS?
THERE'S A FIFTY NOTE IN MY WATCHPOCKET IF YOU CAN. AND A RONCO EXIT-WOUND-O-MATIC IN THE OTHER IF YOU CAN'T.

"SINCE YOU PUT IT LIKE THAT, EFFENDI, I CAN EVEN GIVE YOU HIS PUKIN' SHOESIZE.
"THE MOZART APARTMENTS, BEHIND THE TIERGARTEN. RIGHT UNDER THE FLIGHT-PATH OF THE ORBITALS. HE HAS A ROOM ON THE FOURTH."
"FLOPPY, I WANT YOUR CHILDREN."
FFFCHOOOM!
HEY-SHES CHRISTMAS ON A BIKE! HOW CAN YOU LIVE WITH THAT NOISE?
MONDO

LOW RENT. LOOK- PLEASE- WHO ARE YOU GUYS?
US? WE'RE ICE-HEARTED PISTOLEROS FROM THE MURDERVERSE, WITH CHALK OUT-LINES ROUND OUR SOULS!
SAD

I CAN'T SAY THAT ACTUALLY HELPS. HAVE YOU BEEN PAID TO HURT ME?

NO.
WE DO THAT FOR FREE. WE'VE BEEN PAID TO KILL YOU, GNOME.

KILL ME? KILL ME? FOR PUKESAKES... WHAT HAVE I DONE TO DESERVE THAT?
YOUR GUIDE TO CYBERSEX!

ASK CYBERBILITY BROWN. HE PUT OUT THE MARK. BROWN'S THE MOST FASHIONABLE CYBERSPACE LANDSCAPE ARTIST IN THE CONURB, CORRECT ME IF I'M WRONG.
BUILDS VIRTUAL LANDSCAPES FOR ALL THE TOP CORPORATIONS SO THEIR DATASPHERE DEALINGS CAN BE CONDUCTED IN THE SNAZZIEST ENVIRONMENTS.

SELF-REPLICATING GARDEN GNOMES THAT INVADE HIS VIRTUAL LANDSCAPES AND OVER-WHELM THEM! YOU TOTAL SADIST!
AND YOU SCREW THEM UP! YOU TRASH BILLIONS OF DOLLARS OF HIS WORK!
WHAT DID YOU EXPECT? A PAT ON THE HEAD?

I DIDN'T EXPECT TO DIE FOR IT! IT'S JUST FREE-DOM OF EXPRESSION! A RAGE AGAINST THE MACHINE! A BLOW TO THE SYSTEM!
DOESN'T THAT MEAN ANYTHING TO YOU?
SOB!
YOUR GUIDE TO CYBERSEX!

NO.

FWHAMM!
love bundle
GNOME? ARE YOU OKAY?
WE WERE JUST PRACTISING DOWNSTAIRS AND WE HEARD THE FUSS. ARE THESE PUKES BOTHERING YOU?

OH, THANK GOD KURT! THEY WANT TO KILL ME!
BLUB!
THAT SO? I DON'T THINK SO, SOMEHOW.
SHHUKK!
CCCHHK!
BIO-WEAPONS. IMPLANTS. TESTO-STERONE. CHEERS, GOD!
YAAAAAGH!
DIVE...
SPIN...
LAND...
BLAMBLAMBLAMBLAM!
COOL!

OH MY GOD...
IT'S A GIFT HE HAS.
TWITCH!
TWITCH!

C-CAN'T YOU FORGET ABOUT ME? I'LL LEAVE TOWN! I'LL DO ANYTHING!
WEEEELLL... WE'RE PRIMA KILLERINAS, LIKE I TOLD YOU. THE BEST GUN SHARKS MONEY CAN BUY.
WE HAVE A REPUTATION TO UPHOLD.

AND OUR REPUTATION IS... WHEN WE TAKE A JOB, WE DO THE JOB.
NO REGRETS. NO QUESTIONS. NO REFUNDS.
CHK.CHKK!
NOTHING PERSONAL, MATE.

BOOM!
BA-BOOM!
BOOM!

NICE GROUPING.
HE TOOK IT WELL, I THOUGHT. SORTA RESIGNED. I FELT SORRY FOR HIM... I'M A MORAL ANIMAL WHEN ALL'S SAID AND DONE.

AND THE MORAL IS?
DON'T DUMP YOUR GNOMES ON SOMEONE ELSE'S LAWN.
OR SOMETHIN' LIKE THAT.
COOL
THE END

NERVOUS REX

Script: Dan Abnett

Art: David Millgate

Letters: Steve Potter

Originally published in *2000 AD* Prog 981

SINISTER DEXTER

NEW THRILL
NERVOUS REX
AND THIS IS DOWNLODE, THE CITY THAT SLEEPS WITH ONE EYE OPEN.
IT'S TEN FORTY FIVE, CENTRAL EUROPE TIME, AND SOMEONE'S FEELING NERVOUS...

THE NERVOUS THAT THEY'RE FEELING IS ONE NERVOUS REX, A.K.A. REX MONDAY, INFORMATION BROKER, NARK, SNOUT AND PROFESSIONAL LOW LIFE.
AND FOR NERVOUS, IT'S NOT A GOOD FEELING...
KRAKKKKK!
ANGHHK!

BY DOTHE.
Y-YOUB BWOKEN BY DOTH.
BRILLIAND.

AWW, WHADDA SHAME. AN' YOU WUZ SUCH A GOOD-LOOKIN' GEEK BEFORE.
I'M THRU PLAYIN' GAMES WID CHEW, REX. 'FESS UP, BEFORE I HAFTA GET BALLISTIC ON YER ASS.
SCRIPT
DAN ABNETT
ART
DAVID MILLGATE
LETTERS
STEVE POTTER

'TIS WHAT I'VE ALWAYS LIKED ABOUT YA, QUARANTEENO.
THE SHEER POETRY OF YER VOICE.
HUH? WHOZZAT?

FINNIGAN SINISTER!? BUZZ OFF, YA PUKE!
WELL NOW, I'D LOVE T'OBLIGE YOU THERE, SO I WOULD... BUT WHEN I POP ROUND T'SEE ME OLD MATE NERVOUS, AND FIND HIM ON THE RECEIVING END OF A GOIN' OVER AT THE HANDS OF A MONKEY-BOY BRAIN-DONER LIKE KENTON QUARANTEENO, I HAFTA ASK MESELF A QUESTION...

...DO I SHOOT HIM WHERE HE STANDS...
OR DO I LET HIM START RUNNIN' FIRST?

SAY YER PRAYERS, YA FILTHY BOGTROTTER!

"BOGTROTTER"?

"BOGTROTTER"? ME?

"BOGTROTTER"?

BOOOOM!
BA-BOOOOM!
BOOOOM!
I'LL HAVE YA KNOW I'M THE POET LAUREATE OF THE PUKIN' TRAUMA WARD! I'M THE CHOCOLATE FLAKE OF DEATH IMPALING THE CLUSTER-NUT SUNDAE OF YOUR EXISTENCE!
SO I AM.
- MILLGATE

FOOOMMMSHHHH!

DANKTH, DINITHDER.

DON' MENTION IT, CAMPADRE.

HOW MANY FLOORS UP *ARE* WE, ANY HOW?

DIRDY THEBBEN.

HE'LL BE HITTIN' THE GROUND ABOUT NOW THEN.

THUNCH!

AH *YES.* SO WHAT DID HE WANT WITH YOU, ANYWAY?

HE WATH *-snff-* UNDER THE IMPRETHION THAT I WATH THOME *ORACLE* OF *ALL KNOWLEDGE.*

ATHKED ME *-snff-* FOR A TIP ON THE GREY-HOUNDTH LAST WEEK. WATHN'T MY FAULT *BLINKING THTARFITH* DIDN'T WOMP HOME.
HE'D COME ROUND TO GET HITH MONEY BACK.
OH, *GOD.* MY ULTHER'TH THARTING TO ACT UP AGAIN.

NERVOUS... YOU'RE SO *NERVOUS.*
WHAT DID YOU WANT ANYWAY? AND WHERE'TH RAMONE TONIGHT?
HE'S WAITIN' IN THE EDSEL. WATCHING THAT DAMN *HEAD-TV* OF HIS. SOMETHING ON HE DIDN'T WANT TO MISS...

...¡AY! LASSIE! GOOD GIRL!
¡VAYASE! YOU IS ONE *SMART* POOCH!

SO... DID SENOR NERVOUS HAVE THE SMARTS?
HE ALWAYS HAS THE SMARTS. ACCORDING TO NERVOUS, OL' CURT HAD HIS NEW-FACE SURGERY DONE AT PORKY'S CHOP SHOP ON THE ZATSKOI GYRATORY.
MAN, I STILL CAN'T BELIEVE THEY WANT US TO ICE CURT.
VEGI BURGERS
MONDO

OURS IS NOT TO REASON WHY, AMIGO...
...SURE, CURT VILE IS A FELLOW GUN SHARK, AND ONE O' THE FEW WE'D DOFF OUR HATS TO...

BUT HE MADE OFF WITH MOB MONEY, A LADA MOB MONEY. HE'S GOTTA PAY, MAN. THEM'S DE RULES.

GUESS SO. OH WELL, LET'S DROP BY PORKY'S. NERVOUS SAID CURT MIGHT HAFTA CHECK BACK TO MAKE SURE THE GRAFT'S TAKEN BEFORE HE SKIPS TOWN...

OH, MR VILE, SIR!
THE NEW-FACE GRAFT HAS TAKEN BEAUTIFULLY. I'D SAY IT WAS MY BEST EVER WORK.
IT HAD BETTER BE, PORKY, FOR THE MONEY I'M SHELLING OUT ON IT.

GET ME A MIRROR.
I GOT ME A TICKET ON THE OUTBOUND ORBITAL AT TWO, AND I WANNA LOOK MY BEST.

FORGET THE MIRROR, PORKY.
GO LOOK FER A BODY BAG. BETTER YET... JUST *GO* PERIOD.
OH MY GOD! SINISTER AND DEXTER!

PLEASE... *PLEASE!*
I JUST DID WHAT I WAS PAID TO DO!
SCRAM, PORKY. THIS IS A *GUN SHARK* THING.

THANK YOU! OH THANK YOU..!
COMO ESTA, CURT? YOU BEEN ONE *BAAAD* BOY!
HEY, FELLAS! SO THEY HIRED *YOU* PAIR TO BRING ME DOWN, HUH?
I'M *FLATTERED!* ONLY THE *BEST,* RIGHT?

SAVE US THE *BONHOMIE,* CHUM. WE'VE GOT WORK TO–
–*HOLY BLESSED MOTHER OF BABY JESUS HIMSELF!*

SO WHAT D'YOU *THINK,* HUH?
I'VE *ALWAYS* ADMIRED YOU, DEX... YOUR MOVES, YOUR STYLE, YOUR CHUTZPAH.
I FIGURED IF I *HAD* TO HAVE ANOTHER FACE, *YOURS* WOULD BE THE ONE I'D PICK.

NEXT PROG CURL UP AND DIE!

MAX VACTOR

Script: Dan Abnett

Art: Anthony Williams

Colors: Junior Tomlin

Letters: Steve Potter

Originally published in *2000 AD* Prog 984

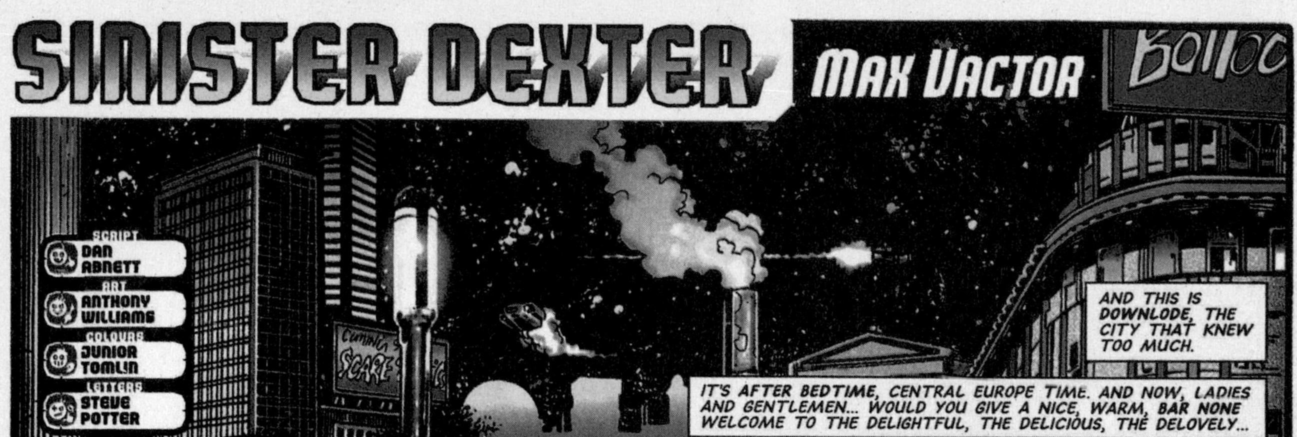

IT'S AFTER BEDTIME, CENTRAL EUROPE TIME. AND NOW, LADIES AND GENTLEMEN... WOULD YOU GIVE A NICE, WARM, BAR NONE WELCOME TO THE DELIGHTFUL, THE DELICIOUS, THE DELOVELY...

...DEMI OCTAVO!

BAR NONE, A SMOKIN' LITTLE NITESPOT OFF SONTAGG STRASSE. EVERY FRIDAY NIGHT AT ELEVEN, **DEMI** SINGS THE BLUES. SHE SINGS THEM SO GOOD, THEY SOUND **TURQUOISE**.

GIVE ME A MAN WITH A GUN IN HIS HAND THERE AIN'T NOTHING THAT THAT MAN CAN'T DO. GIVE ME A JOE WITH HIS HAT PULLED DOWN LOW NO, THERE AIN'T NOTHING THAT THAT MAN CAN'T DO.

CAUSE THAT MAN O' MINE LOOKIN' OH-SO-FINE WHOA, THERE AIN'T NOTHING, NOTHING, NOTHING THAT THAT MAN CAN'T DO
TABLE EIGHT, NEAR THE BACK. THREE COVERS... SINISTER, DEXTER AND THEIR NARK, NERVOUS REX.
OKAY, GENTS! I GOT ONE TEQUILA SUNSET, ONE..um... MILK?
THAT'D BE MINE. THANK YOU.
AND ONE PISTON BROKE?
RIGHT OVER HERE, DARLIN'.

SHOW ME A GUY
WITH THAT LOOK IN HIS EYE
THERE AIN'T NOTHING THAT
THAT MAN CAN'T DO
Ah
ME! DEMI OCTAVO. SUCH STUFF AS DREAMS ARE MADE OF. REGULARLY.
YOU SURE I CAN'T STIFFEN YOUR MILK THERE, REX-ME-BOY?
N-NO, THANKS, SINISTER. M-MILK IS JUST DANDY. I HAVE A N-NERVOUS STOMACH.
DO TELL.

D-DEXTER SEEMS TO BE ENJ-JOYING THE SHOW, ANYWAY...
HIM? NAAH! HES WATCHING HIS HEAD TV AGAIN.
WHAT'S ON TONIGHT, RAMONE?
IT'S DE SEEX MILLION DOLLAR MAN...
SONY

¡AY! ¡VAYASE! DEY CAN REBUILD HIM! DEY DO HAVE DE TECHNOLOGY!

IGNORE HIM! SO WHAT'S THE DEAL, REX? YOU CALLED THIS MEET. YOU GOT A JOB FOR US?
Y-YES. FROM HOLY MOSES HIMSELF. HE D-DIDNT WANT TO USE THE FACT-TOTEM TO HIRE YOU, BECAUSE THE MATTER IS A LITTLE... DELICATE...

...IT C-CONCERNS HIS GIRLFRIEND OVER THERE...
AND I MEAN IT! 'CAUSE I SEEN IT! THERE AIN'T NOTHING THAT THAT MAN CAN'T DO!

THANK YOU.
THANK YOU SO MUCH.
DEMI OCTAVO, LADIES AND GENTLEMEN! LET'S HEAR IT!
YAAAYYY!
WHOOO-WHOOOO!
YAAAHH!

LATER, PROWLING THE VIRCADES AND THE PLAY-PARLOURS OFF THE INTERSTATE SCHNELLWEG...
...SO THE BODACIOUS SENORITA IS PLAYING AWAY?
THAT'S ABOUT THE SIZE OF IT, BUDSTER.
THE LUSCIOUS MISS OCTAVO HAS NOT BEEN... HOW CAN I PUT IT? ...ONE HUNDRED PERCENT MONOGAMOUS OF LATE.
PLAY
PLAY
AND WHEN YER OTHER HALF IS "HOLY" MOSES TANENBAUM, THAT'S A SERIOUSLY DANGEROUS GAME TA PLAY.
¡AY! SHE COULD GET DEAD REAL QUICK, NO QUESTIONS!
IT WOULD BE A SHAME THOUGH... WHAT A VOICE... WHAT A BOD!
MAX MOTION
in
MECHISMO DESPERADO
"Top bloke!" CineNet
"I was so excited I wet me kecks" Variety
MAX MOTION? MAX MOTION?
DOESN'T EVERYONE?
OH. THAT MAX MOTION.
THAT'S CLEARLY WHAT MOSES THINKS TOO! NO POINT IN SMOKING A WORK OF ART LIKE DEMI!
SO WE GET TO SMOKE HER SIDE SQUEEZE INSTEAD.
ACCORDING TO REX, THE PUKE'S NAME IS MAX MOTION. HE'S A VACTOR.
YOU KNOW HIM, EFFENDI?

SMILE WHEN YOU CALL ME THAT, BABY.
OH MAX!
Mmfff!
AND CUT!
HOW WAS IT, ORSS?
GREAT, MAXIE, GREAT PASH, GREAT SMOULDER.
WILL SOMEBODY KILL THE VIRT?
ORSS
VIRRWWHT!
THANK YOU, LOVES.
NOW LET'S TAKE A BREAKETTE. IF I DON'T GET SOME BRIOCHE INSIDE ME SOON, IT'LL BE HELLO HYPOGLYCAEMIA!
YOU SURE THAT WENT OKAY, ORSS?
ORSS
WELL, WE'RE NOT SISKEL AND EBERT, BUT WE THOUGHT IT SUCKED.
WHO THE PUKE ARE YOU? HOW DID YOU GET ON-SET?
CAREFUL, ORSS! THEY LOOK LIKE THEY COULD BE VERY HEAVY!
"ORSS"? WHAT KIND OF NAME IS "ORSS"?
IT'S SHORT FOR... FOR... ORSON. MY CHRISTIAN NAME.
WHAT'S YOUR SURNAME?
PENISTONE.
FANCY.

WHICH OF YOU IS MAX MOTION?
I AM.
WHAT'S IT TO YOU?

FIFTEEN HUNDRED IN UNMARKED BILLS.
EVERYBODY TAKE A LONG LUNCH.
LOOSE THE VIRT HAT, MOTION.

BROTHER! DO YOU LOOK BETTER ON SCREEN!
I'M A VACTOR, WHAT DO YOU EXPECT?
THEY MAP MY LOOKS ONTO ME IN P.P.
WHY D'YOU THINK I NEVER LOOK THE SAME FROM FILM TO FILM?

WELL, I GOT A RADICAL NEW LOOK FOR YOUR NEXT V-LICK...
...STIFF, PALE, WITH A TOUCH OF LIVIDITY AND MORE THAN THE USUAL NUMBER OF ORIFICES.
K-CCHAKK!
AAHHH! WHY! WHY ARE YOU DOING THIS?

YOU BIN PARKIN' YOUR FLIP-FLOPS UNDER ANOTHER MAN'S FUTON, MAXIE-BOY.
AND THAT MAN HAPPENS TO BE THE BIG HOLY ONE, GODFATHER O' DOWNLODE.
WHICH IN TURN MAKES YOU VERY POST-ALIVE INDEED. WE'RE HERE TO DELIVER A COMMUNIQUE FROM CUCKOLDEE TO CUCKOLDER.

ONE THING I GOTTA KNOW... HOW DOES A PUKE LIKE YOU HOOK AN UBER-FOX LIKE DEMI OCTAVO?
OH, TYPICAL! YOU'RE SO SUPERFICIAL! LOOKS AREN'T EVERYTHING, YOU KNOW!
DEMI SAYS I HAVE INNER BEAUTY.

NEXT PROG DEATH & TAXIS!

DEATH AND TAXIS

Script: Dan Abnett

Art: Charles Gillespie

Letters: Steve Potter

Originally published in *2000 AD* Prog 985

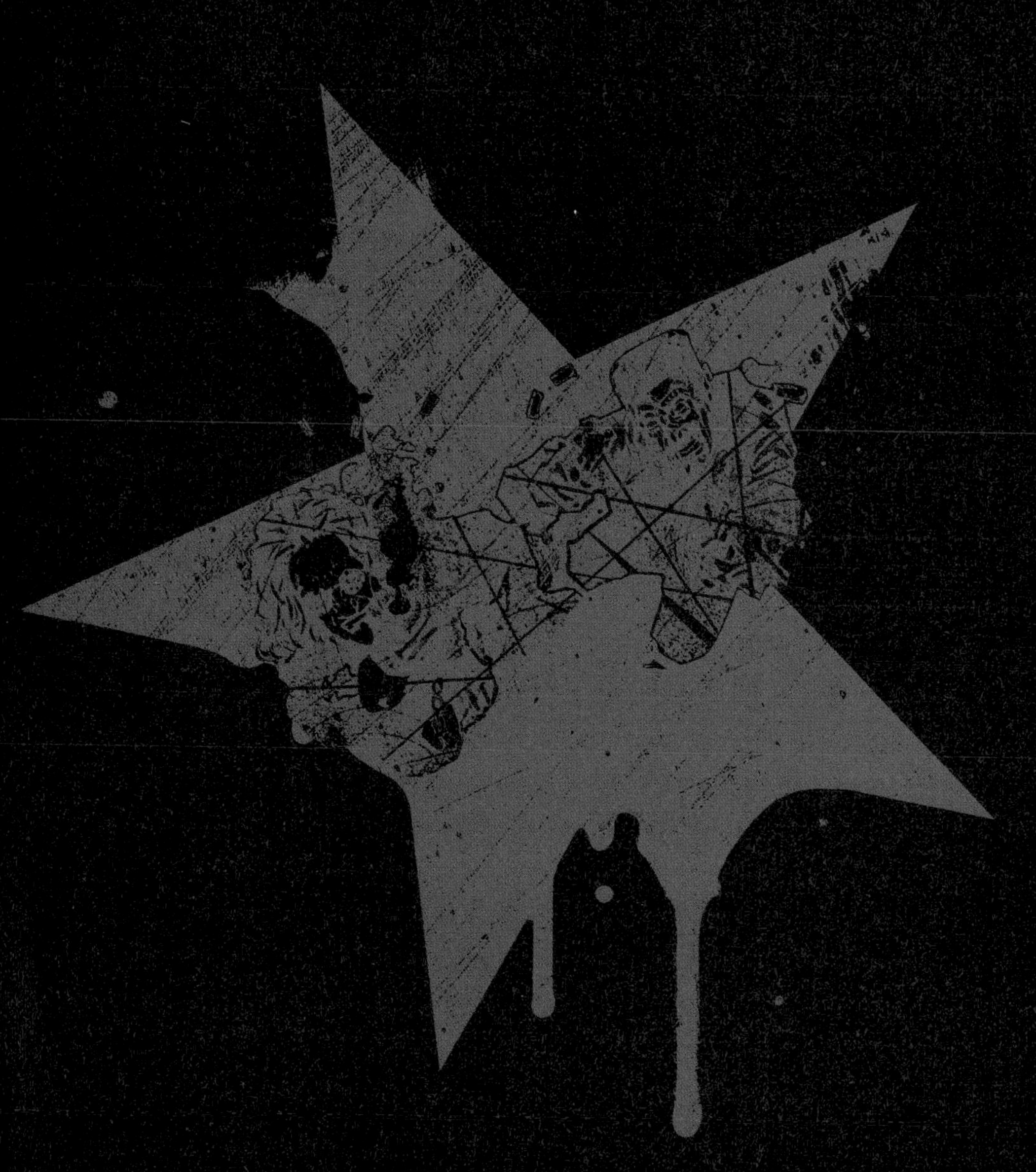

SINISTER DEXTER

SINISTER DEXTER Death & Taxis

AND THIS IS DOWNLODE, THE CITY THAT CALLED WHILE YOU WERE OUT.
EIGHT AFTER TEN, CENTRAL EUROPE TIME. RUSALKA PROSPECT. NEIGHBOURS REPORT SHOTS...
BURGERS
SLOW DOWN NOW

ZOOB! ZOOB! ZOOB! ZOOB!
UNIT ELEVEN EIGHTY RESPONDING.
HOTEL
SCRIPT DAN ABNETT
ART CHARLES GILLESPIE
LETTERS STEVE POTTER

ZOOB! ZOOB! ZOOB! ZO-*
CAN THE HOOTER. SEE ANYTHING?
THE BIG ZIPPETY-DON'T-DA.

LET'S SPLIT.
SHOULD WE CHECK THAT CAB?
DO I LOOK LIKE I WANNA CHECK THAT CAB?

WHERE TO, GENT'S?
SPANISHVILLE, PAL.
AND YOU MAY DEPRESS THE THROTTLE WITH UTMOST ALACRITY.

STEP ON IT, RIGHT?
IN A NUTSHELL.

DEXTER! KEEP HIM UPRIGHT FER PUKESAKES!
¡VAYASE! HE'S GONE ALL BENDY.
HE WAS OKAY AT STANDIN' UP FOR HIMSELF UNTIL YOU SHOT HIM.

JUST PROP HIM VERTICAL TIL RIGOR TAKES UP THE SLACK.
HEY-SUES H! THIS LITTLE CAPER IS NOT GOING ACCORDING TO PLAN!

NOT MY FAULT.
STOP SULKING. AND IT WAS YOUR FAULT.
SEZ YOU.
OKAY, OKAY... WHO FORGOT WHERE HE PARKED THE CAR? HUH? HUH? WHO FORGOT TO BRING A SILENCER? TELL ME THAT?

SO, YOU OUT FOR THE EVENING, GENTS? LOOKING FOR A GOOD TIME?
STARTED EARLY, I'D SAY. YOUR FRIEND THERE LOOKS A LITTLE THE WORSE FOR WEAR, KNOW WHAT I MEAN?
TELL HIM SOMETHING, DEX. MAKE SOMETHING UP.

ACTUALLY, SENOR, OUR FRIEND HERE IS... IS...
PARALYSED
...PARALYSED ...WITH JOY BECAUSE HE'S GETTING MARRIED IN THE MORNING TO...TO...
TO THE STRAINS OF MENDELS-SON
...TO THE STRAINS OF MENDELSSON AND... AND THIS IS HIS LAST NIGHT OF... OF...
OF THE ROUND TABLE
HA HAA!
SURE HE IS. LISTEN, GENTS, YOU GET IN THE BACK OF MY CAB, YOU GOT CLIENT CONFIDENTIALITY. I BEEN ROUND THE BLOCK A FEW TIMES, I SEEN THE WORLD FOR WHAT IT IS.
SO COME ON... WHAT'S THE REAL STORY HERE, HUH?
OKAY.
WE'RE GUN SHARKS. WE HAVE JUST KILLED THIS MAN. BY THE TERMS OF OUR CONTRACT, WE HAVE TO GET HIS BONES TO AN ADDRESS IN SPANISHVILLE AS PROOF OF DEATH.
WE LOUSED UP OUR GETAWAY SO WE HAILED YOUR CAB. APART FROM THE COPS, THIS MAN'S EMPLOYEES MAY BE AFTER US TO GET RETRIBUTION.
Errrmm... YUP! THAT'S ABOUT THE SIZE OF IT.
SSKKEEEECHK!
HEY! HEY, WAIT!
LISTEN TO ME, RAMONE...
...THE TRUTH IS LIKE A BOX O' CHOCOLATES. A BITE IS NICE, BUT EAT THE WHOLE LOT AND YOU'LL BE ILL DOWN YOUR SLACKS.

OY! SPANK ME!
SPANG!
SPEOW!
SOME BOLUS-BRAIN IS SHOOTIN' AT US, ALREADY!
POW!
TRES GUESSES WHO, AMIGO!
SMASSH!

"IT'S THE STIFF'S COMPADRES!"

POUR IT ON, EFFENDI! THESE TOTAL PUKEHOLES ARE WAZZING ME OFF!
¡AY! YOU GOT THAT RIGHT!
BAMM!
BAMM!
BOOM!

DAWN, SPANISHVILLE...
CHK-CHK-CHK BANG! CHK-CHK-CHK!

PULL IT OVER HERE, DEX.
CHK-CHK-CHK-CHK BANG! CHK-CHK-CHK!

THIS IS THE PLACE, FIFTEEN BOMBONES STREET.
AT LAST...
YOU IN THE CAB! STEP OUT NOW!

OH PUKE.

¡HOLA! CAN WE HELP YOU, OFFICERS?
YOU HAVE MUFFLER DAMAGE. GET IT REPAIRED IN THE NEXT EIGHT DAYS...
...OR THERE'LL BE TROUBLE.

NEXT PROG FINNIGAN'S MINIGUN!

SINISTER DEXTER

THE ELEVENTH COMMANDMENT

Script: Dan Abnett

Art: Charles Gillespie

Letters: Steve Potter

Originally published in *2000 AD* Progs 988 - 989

SINISTER DEXTER
THE ELEVENTH COMMANDMENT PART 1
AND THIS IS DOWNLOAD, THE CITY THAT SHOULD HAVE CHANGED THOSE STUPID LOCKS.
IT'S CLOSE TO A.M., CENTRAL EUROPE TIME, AND SOMETHING VERY BIG IS ABOUT TO GO DOWN.
LET'S SWING OUT WEST, PAST IMELDA PROSPEKCT, TO THE OBSCENE WEALTH NEIGHBOURHOOD...
SCRIPT DAN ABNETT
ART CHARLES GILLESPIE
LETTERS STEVE POTTER

...AND A DES RES CALLED MOUNT OLIVE.
WE KNOW WHO LIVES HERE, RIGHT?
MR TANENBAUM? THE MEN YOU SENT FOR ARE HERE.
Y-HUH... HOLY MOSES TANENBAUM, THE GODFATHER OF DOWNLODE.

ROD. GOOD OF YOU TO COME. I SEE YOU'VE BROUGHT YOUR STAFF.
YES, THEY'RE ALL HERE, SIR.

GOOD, GOOD.
WELL, ROD. IT'S A BLACK DAY. I WOULDN'T HAVE SENT FOR YOU OTHERWISE.
YOU KNOW THE SCORE HERE. I WANT THINGS SETTLED. WE'LL SAY TRIPLE RATES, PLUS THE USUAL BONUS.

GENEROUS, MR TANENBAUM, SIR.
BUT SURELY NOT NECESSARY?
NO ONE WOULD BE CRAZY ENOUGH TO TAKE THIS C-
"THEY" WOULD.
THEY WOULD HAVE NO CHOICE. IT'S THEIR REPUTATION, YOU UNDERSTAND, ROD, AN HONOUR THING.
I KNOW THEM. THEY'RE LIKE SONS TO ME. THEY'RE THE BEST GUN SHARKS MONEY CAN BUY.
AND THEY WILL COME, BECAUSE THAT IS WHAT THEY DO. THEY MUST COME, BECAUSE THAT IS WHAT THEY ARE. TO TURN ASIDE WOULD BE FAILURE.
IT BREAKS MY HEART THAT THIS IS SO, AND MAKES ME REJOICE AT THE SAME TIME. SUCH PROFESSIONALS.
I UNDERSTAND, HOLY ONE. SO WHAT'S THE GOOD WORD?
THY ROD & STAFF ARE HERE TO COMFORT YOU.
R-CHKKK!
RACHIKK!
R-CHKKK!
THE ELEVENTH COMMANDMENT, ROD.
THOU SHALT NOT SUFFER FINNIGAN SINISTER OR RAMONE DEXTER TO LIVE.
AMEN.

CUT EAST, PAST THE LIFTER 'BURBS AND THE SOFTWARE WHARFS, ACROSS THE CHATTERING VIRCADES AND THE WAR MEMORIALS ON ZONTIK CIRCLE...
...TO LONELY DONEGAN'S EATERIA...
Lonely Donegan's

...AND A MOMENT OF PERFECT CALM.
RAMONE ALGONQUIN WINNEBAGO DEXTER. CASUAL KILLER. GUN SHARK.
HIS MIDDLE NAMES CELEBRATE, RESPECTIVELY, THE SITE OF HIS CONCEPTION AND THE PLACE OF HIS BIRTH. TO WIT, THE ALGONQUIN HOTEL AND A WINNEBAGO TRAILER.

TWO MONTHS AGO, RAMONE BOUGHT A HEADCASE TV™ AND HAD IT IMPLANTED IN HIS PINEAL GLAND IN A CHOP SHOP UP WEST.
NOW PRIME TIME REPEATS AND MOVIE-THON EPICS ARE BEAMED DIRECTLY INTO HIS MIND, TWENTY FOUR HOURS A DAY.
¡AY!
¡VAYASE!
RUN, RAQUEL, RUN! THAT FURRY GEE-STRING AIN'T GONNA STOP NO ALLOSAUR CHOMP!

ENTER HIS PARTNER, FINNIGAN SINISTER, THE LAST OF THE LYRICAL GANGSTAS.
HEY, DEX!
NOT NOW, PARD. I'M IN DYNAMATION HEAVEN!

THEN CONSIDER THIS A PASSPORT BACK TO STOP-MOTION HELL.
THE KAKA AN' THE FAN JUST HAD MEANINGFUL INTERCOURSE, EFFENDI.
KLAKK!

NO WAY!
THIS... THIS *CAN'T* BE RIGHT! THE FACT-TOTEM MUST BE WRONG!

OH, IT'S *RIGHT*, ALL RIGHT. SOMEONE'S PUT A CONTRACT OUT...
...ON *HOLY MOSES*.
WHICH GIVES THEE AND ME A *CHOICE*...

IGNORE IT AND DESTROY OUR REP AS THE HOTTEST KILL-BOYS THERE EVER WAS...
OR *TAKE* IT AND BITE THE HAND THAT FEEDS US.
¡VAYASE! IT'S THE RULES! IT'S OUR CODE! WE *ALWAYS* TAKE THE JOB...

BUT *BAG THE HOLY ONE?* I SAY WE F-
DEX! KISS THE CARPET! NOW!

JAYCEASE HAITCH CHRISTENDOM ON A TWO-STROKE RICKSHAW!
THUNK
THUNK
THUNK
THUNK

MOTHER O' PUKIN' MERCY! IT'S ROD & HIS STAFF! WHAT'RE THEY DOIN' TRYING TA PLUG US?
SPREAD OUT. I WANT THESE KILLS CONFIRMED.
WHO CARES, AMIGO?
QUESTION IS... DO WE DANCE?

DOES THE POPE DRIVE A FISH-TANK?
'COURSE WE DANCE!
I HEAR THAT! DRILL THE SCUZZ-PUCKS!
BOOM!
BOOM!
BAMM!
BAMM-BAMM!
CHA-BOOM!
BAMM!

THEY'RE STILL WARM! POUR IT ON!
yerk!

YOU PUKEHOLES MADE A SERIOUS LIFE-ERROR ROLLING IN ON US!
WE'RE DEAD-EYED LEAD-SOWERS FROM THE BANKS OF THE STYX AND OUR GUNS ARE ALWAYS HUNGRY! YOU DON'T BE MESSIN' WITH US!
eghhkk!

DAMN THAT MOSES! THIS AIN'T NO PROMISED LAND!
GET OUT! DISENGAGE AND GET OUT!
aghh!

NEXT PROG PATRIARCH GAMES!

SINISTER DEXTER

THE ELEVENTH COMMANDMENT

PART 2

FOR RAMONE DEXTER, IT'S BEEN A MONDO STINKO NIGHT. THE WATCHBOT SENTRIES ON THE MANSION'S OUTER WALLS WERE PEASY TARGETS. SO WERE THE GUNSELS ON THE PORCH STEPS.

HIS TWIN CHROME AUTO-NINES CHEWED THROUGH THE SECOND RANK OF TORPEDOES WAITING IN THE FOYER.

Uuh...Uuh... Uuh...Uuh...

SCRIPT DAN ABNETT
ART CHARLES GILLESPIE
LETTERS STEVE POTTER

THEN SOMEONE... SOMEONE WHO KNEW HE HAD A HEADCASE TV SURGICALLY GRAFTED INTO HIS PINEAL GLAND, TURNED ON SOME KIND OF E-MAG DISRUPTOR AND ZAPPED HIS BRAIN VIA THE IMPLANT FEED.
TEN SECONDS AGO HE WAS ONE OF THE BEST GUN SHARKS MONEY COULD BUY.
...Uuh...Uuh... H-HOLY KID OF G-GOD... WHITE NOISE, IN MY HEAD, H-HURTING LIKE A SONOVABISH...

NOW HE'S LOOKING AT A GREAT CAREER IN DROOLING.
...SINISTER? OIGA, SINISTER... YOU THERE, AMIGO?
H- HELP ME, POR FAVOR. IT HURT SO MUCH, AND I CAN'T SEE NOTHING NO MORE... SINISTER?

FINNIGAN SINISTER, THE OTHER HALF OF THE DUO.
FLIGHT UP, LOADED FOR ARMOUR-CLAD BEAR, TRYING TO IGNORE HIS PARTNER'S AGONISED PLEAS FLOATING UP FROM THE STAIRWELL.
FOOOOM!
"THIS KAKA", FOR THOSE OF YOU TAKING YOUR SEATS LATE AND RUSTLING YOUR DAMN POPCORN, IS AS FOLLOWS...
Eiiiigggggggh!
SOME PUKING FOOL HAS PUT OUT A CONTRACT ON DOWNLODE'S IMPERIAL GANGSTA, HOLY MOSES TANENBAUM.
FOOOOM!
Tut tut! HEARD YER THUMB ON THE HAMMER!
I HEAR YA, BUD. I'LL BE BACK FOR YA SOON AS THIS KAKA IS OVER WITH...
gehgggh!
YA-THOOOM!
AND YOU GOT THE LOUDEST SHOES IN CHRISTEN-DOM!
MOSES? YA HEAR ME, Y'FEARFUL OLD PATRIARCH?
TIS FINNIGAN SINISTER HERE. MOSES! WE GOT US SOME BIG STUFF TO SETTLE!
WHICH MEANS THE CITY'S BEST GUNS-U-HIRE HAVE BECOME VOCATIONALLY OBLIGATED TO STOP BY MOUNT OLIVE, THE BIG HOLY ONE'S PALATIAL HOME, AND GET ALL PROFESSIONAL ON HIM.
IT'S A REPUTATON THING, SEE?
OF COURSE WE DO, FINNIGAN. STEP INSIDE, MY FRIEND. WE'LL TALK.
COME ON IN, SON. LET'S NOT PROLONG THIS.

MOSES? SHOW YERSELF, BIG GUY, OR I START SOWING WILD WITH ME CANNON SET TO SCATTER.

HERE I AM, OLD FRIEND.
I'VE BEEN WAITING. I KNEW YOU'D COME.
KLKK!

WE HAD TA TAKE THE MARK, MOSES. TIS WHAT WE *DO*.
Y'UNDERSTAND, DONCHA? TIS NOTHIN' *PERSONAL*.

OF COURSE NOT, SON, I'D HAVE FELT BETRAYED IF YOU *HADN'T* TAKEN THE CONTRACT.
WHAT'VE I ALWAYS SAID? "SINISTER AND DEXTER..? BEST BODYCOUNTERS IN THE BOOK?" LAW OF THE URBAN JUNGLE, MY FRIEND.
BUT IT'S COST US BOTH. YOU CUT MY HOUSEHOLD STAFF TO SHREDS, AND ONLY *ONE* OF YOU MADE IT UP THE STAIRS. WE'RE ALMOST EVEN. *ALMOST*.
NOW I THINK IT'S TIME WE FINISHED THIS, DON'T YOU?

FBAMMMCHHH!
Y'HUH! WHY NOT!
OH SHUG. I SHOULDA GUESSED A WEALTH MAGNET LIKE YOU WOULD BE PERSONALLY SHIELDED.
OF COURSE. A LITTLE HARD-LIGHT BODY SCREEN, STATE OF THE ART MILITARY HARDWARE.
AND IT WORKS JUST SWELL. ALL ROUND INVISIBLE BALLISTIC PROTECTION, EXCEPT FOR ONE SMALL HOLE...
...DESIGNED TO FIT MY GUN BARREL.
GOODBYE, FINNIGAN.
BLAM
AYHUG!
FINNIGAN? OH, MAN.

ehykk?

F-BAMMM

...I WAS BLIND, BUT NOW I SEE.

YOU HANG ON, AMIGO... I GET YOU TO SOME FINE SAWBONES PRONTO, FIX YOU UP GOOD...

...sure, sure...tell me, bro... how'd you do that?

MOSES FRIED MY HEADCASE WITH A MAG PULSE. TOTALLY LOST PICTURE QUALITY AND WORSE, I GOT BLOOD OUT THE EARS...

...*BUT,* WHEN I COME ROUND, I FIND I CAN SEE *INFRA RED.* MY OPTIC IMPLANTS ARE PICKING THINGS UP OFF THE SCALE. I COULD *SEE* HIS BODY SHIELD.

SO I POPPED MY ROUND THROUGH HIS LITTLE BITTY GUN HOLE.

...Heh! That's *special,* mate...

SO, IT'S OVER? YOU GOT THE BIG HOLY *RAT?*

MISS OCTAVO? YOU SAY THAT LIKE... IT WAS *YOU* WHO... WHO...

THE CONTRACT WAS MINE. I WANTED HIM DEAD.

AFTER ALL HE DID TO ME. HE HAD MY LOVER KILLED. HE REALLY SCREWED UP MY LIFE.

Y'KNOW? THEY WERE RIGHT ABOUT YOU TWO, RAMONE...

"...YOU ARE THE BEST GUN SHARKS MONEY CAN BUY."

...gee... always knew that broad would be bad news for Moses one day. You think we shoulda told her it was *us* what iced her squeeze?

NO. NOW SHUT UP. SAVE YOUR STRENGTH. I'M GONNA GET YOU TO THAT DOC, AND YOU AIN'T GONNA DO NO DYIN' ON ME...

...AND DON'T GET NO BLOOD ON THE UPHOLSTERY NEITHER...
AND THIS IS DOWNLODE, THE CITY THAT DANCED THE WHOLE NIGHT THROUGH.
IT'S THE FAR SIDE OF MIDNIGHT, CENTRAL EUROPE TIME AND RAMONE DEXTER SLIDES THE EDSEL INTO THE WESTBOUND LANE OF THE BLEVMOI EXPRESSWAY...
...AND DRIVES TOWARDS ANOTHER DAY.

NEXT PROG **THE ALIBI OF BROADWAY!**

ALIBI OF BROADWAY

Script: Dan Abnett

Art: Charles Gillespie

Letters: Steve Potter

Originally published in *2000 AD* Progs 990 - 991

SINISTER DEXTER

AND THIS IS DOWNLODE, THE CITY THAT COULDN'T GET NO SATISFACTION.
IT'S WAY PAST CARING, CENTRAL EUROPE TIME, AND DOWN ON SONTAG STRASSE, TWO LIVES ARE ABOUT TO COLLIDE HEAD ON...
ALIBI OF BROADWAY
PART 1

WATCH YOUR DRIVING, YOU FLOB-BRAINED WAZZER! WE'RE GOING TO-!
0000PS 2

SCRIPT
DAN ABNETT
ART
CHARLES GILLESPIE
LETTERS
STEVE POTTER
KRANNG!
I DO NOT BELIEVE YOU DONE THIS! I HAD PUKIN' RIGHT OF WAY YOU BARF-GARGLE GROLLY-SACK!

LANGUAGE.
K-BLAMM!

WELL?
SHE'S BAILED, KAISER. MUST'VE RUN FOR IT.

MOST LIKELY GONE TO GROUND IN ONE OF THE NEIGHBOURHOOD DIVES.
SPREAD OUT. CHECK THEM. FIND THAT CHEATING WITCH.
PEEK
BAR

AND BRING ME HER *SEVERED HEAD* IN AN *ICE BUCKET*.

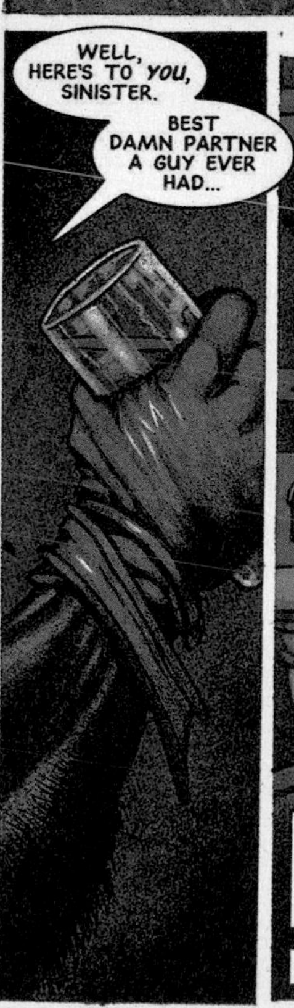
WELL, HERE'S TO *YOU*, SINISTER.
BEST DAMN PARTNER A GUY EVER HAD...

...MAY YOU *REST IN PEACE*.
THE BAR NONE, JUST OFF THE STRIP. IT'S A SLOW NIGHT, A TIME THE STAFF CALL "UNHAPPY HOUR". WHERE EVERY SHMUCK HAS A BROKEN HEART TO NUMB OR A SORROW TO DROWN.
WITNESS... RAMONE DEXTER.
REAL

¡VAYASE! I MISS THE OLD SONOVAPUKE ALREADY...
FIRST SIGN OF MADNESS.

TALKING TO YOURSELF, SPORT. VERY DEFINITELY THE FIRST SIGN OF INCIPIENT BARKINGDOM.
¿COMO DICE? WHAT IS?
I SEE. THERE WOULD BE OTHER SIGNS, LATER ON?
SURE. DROOLING, UNDERTAKING MURALS WITH YOUR OWN–
AHH, THERE YOU ARE, BARMAN! CAN I GET A SOUR JACKIE-O WITH JUST A JIGGER OF LIME? BIG THANKS.
SO... YOU DRINKING TO FORGET... OR CAN'T YOU REMEMBER?
SENORA, IT'S BEEN A ROUGH WEEK. WHAT CAN I SAY? MY PARTNER GOT HIMSELF SHOT.
TOOK A SOFTNOSE THROUGH THE CHESTAL CAVITY. AY! THERE WAS SOME BIG MESS, I CAN TELL YOU.
SSHH! SEE THAT GUY WHO JUST WALKED BY? REAL PERVY TYPE? I ONLY CAME IN HERE BECAUSE I THOUGHT HE WAS FOLLOWING ME.
RELAX, SENORA. I'LL GET RID OF HIM.
APPLY THE BRAKES, AMIGO. TWO THINGS YOU SHOULD KNOW...
...YOUR AFTERSHAVE MAKES THE SENORA HEAVE. AND I AM A PROFESSIONAL KILLER WITH LITTLE OR NO PATIENCE.
NOW BUG OFF.

KCHAKK!
no guns... no guns!
NO WAY, "JOSE". DON'T CARE IF YOU'RE *SPEEDY GON-PUKING-ZALES*, YOU CAN'T OUTDRAW A GUN TO YOUR *SKULL*.
SO WHAT'S GONNA *HAPPEN* IS YOU'RE GONNA GET REAL *LOST* AND LEAVE THE LADY TO ME.
SENOR, YOU LOOK UP "FAST" IN THE DICTIONARY, YOU SEE A PICTURE OF *MY FACE*.
BAMMM!
GHAHKK!
Ahhhh! PLEASE! *PLEASE*, DON'T-
HEY, IT IS *YOUR* FINGER ON THE TRIGGER, AMIGO.

NOW LOOK WHAT YOU DID.
BAMMFF!

THAT WAS TRULY THE MOST *AMAZINGLY* FAST THING I HAVE *EVER* SEEN.
HEARD YOU SAY YOU WERE A *GUN SHARK*. YOU GOT AN *HOURLY RATE?*

SHE SAYS HER NAME IS MELODY BROADWAY.
SHE TELLS HIM SHE'S IN TROUBLE FROM A CRAZY EX-LOVER WHO WON'T GIVE UP. SHE EXPLAINS SHE CAN'T PAY HIM.
HE TELLS HER HE'LL DO IT FOR FREE.
I NEED TO GET OUT OF TOWN. IF I CAN GET ONTO THE SIX AM TRANSCONTINENTAL, I'M SAFE. I CAN KISS THIS STINKING PLACE GOODBYE.
WE CAN MAKE THAT. NO PROBLEM.
WHY ARE YOU HELPING ME, SPORT? THERE'S NO MONEY IN THIS, AND YOU COULD GET HIGHLY DEAD.
CLEVER ANSWER? EVER SINCE MY PARTNER TOOK THAT SLUG, I BEEN LOOKING AT MY LIFE REAL HARD. AND I FIGURE MAYBE THERE ARE MORE IMPORTANT THINGS THAN FOLDING GREEN.
DUMB ANSWER? BECAUSE YOU SURE ARE THE MOST BEAUTIFUL GIRL I EVER SEEN.
Oh.
WHO SHOT YOUR PARTNER, DEX?
MOSES TANENBAUM, THE GANGLORD. WE'D BEEN HIRED TO KILL HIM AND–
–UH OH.
SHREEEEEEEEKKK!

NEXT PROG **OFF BROADWAY!**

SINISTER DEXTER

ALIBI OF BROADWAY PART 2

AND THIS IS DOWNLODE, THE CIT THAT HAS ITS MOTHER'S EYES.

IT'S SO LATE IT'S EARLY, CENTRAL EUROPE TIME, AN DOWN ON THE RAIN-SWABBED DRACHEN EXPRESSWAY DEATH IS PSYCHOTIC AND DRIVES A RED LIMO...

LITTLE BABY JESUS! WE ARE GONNA BE SO DEAD ANY SECOND!
SPRANG!
PANG!
TPOW!
IN THE FIRING LINE... GUN SHARK RAMONE DEXTER AND THE SWEET GIRL HE THOUGHT IT WOULD BE FUN TO PROTECT, ONE MELODY BROADWAY.

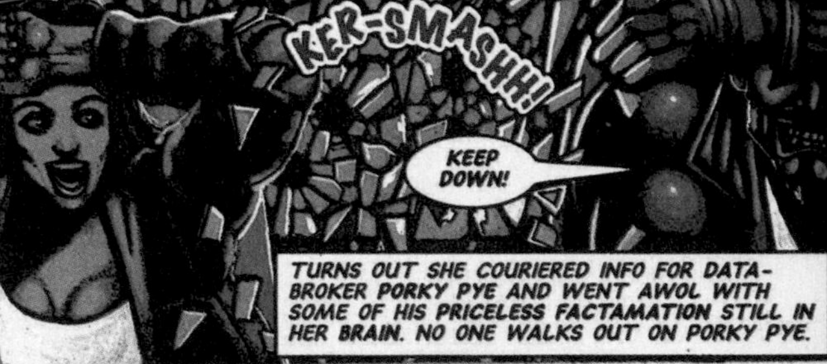

KER-SMASHH!
KEEP DOWN!
TURNS OUT SHE COURIERED INFO FOR DATA-BROKER PORKY PYE AND WENT AWOL WITH SOME OF HIS PRICELESS FACTAMATION STILL IN HER BRAIN. NO ONE WALKS OUT ON PORKY PYE.

BRRRRAAAAPPPPPP!
THIS IS KAISER, A MURDER-ADDICTED NUTTER AND THE CHIEF TORPEDO ON PYE'S PAYROLL.
GONNA MAKE YOU BLEED, CHEAT-WITCH! AND YOUR BOYFRIEND TOO!
SCRIPT DAN ABNETT
ART CHARLES GILLESPIE
LETTERS STEVE POTTER

THUKK!
SPANG-
WE HAVE GOT TO SHAKE HIM OFF!
THERE'S AN EXIT LANE COMING UP...

THERE'S A DIRTY GREAT ROAD TRAIN COMING UP THE INSIDE!
I KNOW. STAY DOWN, SENORA.

BRRMMM---FPASSSHHHHTTT!

I DON'T BELIEVE WHAT YOU JUST DID...
WAS THAT WAY COOL OR WAS THAT WAY COOL?
KAISER'LL HAVE TO WAIT TILL THE NEXT JUNCTION TO GET OFF THE EXPRESS-WAY. WE BOUGHT US SOME BREATHING SPACE.

WE'LL DITCH THE EDSEL HERE. GO ON FOOT FOR A WHILE.
YOUR POOR CAR. YOU LOVED IT, DIDN'T YOU?
HEY, WE'RE ALIVE! THAT'S THE IMPORTANT THING. 'SIDES, I ALWAYS WANTED A CONVERTIBLE.

OPTIMIST. SAVIOUR. HEART-BREAKER. YOU'RE QUITE A GUY, RAMONE DEXTER.
Heh! VAYASE.

IT'S KAISER, MR PYE. YU-HUH. MELODY SHOOK US OFF AT FEEDER NINE. WE'RE DOUBLING BACK.
SHE'S LATCHED ON TO A TRIGGER-PUPPY CALLED DEXTER. YU-HUH, *THAT* DEXTER.
OKAY, YOU COULD *TRY* THAT. BUT I'M ON TOP OF IT.
ANOTHER *HOUR* TOPS AND SHE'LL BE COLLECTING HER THOUGHTS WITH A *SPOON*.
...ANOTHER HALF KLICK, WE'LL BE INTO GOPPINGEN. FROM THERE ITS A SHORT HOP TO THE INTERCONTINENTAL EISENBAHN AT FLUGE.
GOD, YOU REALLY *KNOW* THIS CITY, DON'T YOU?
ALL MY LIFE, I'VE LIVED HERE. SLEPT HERE. *KILLED* HERE.
CAN I ASK YOU A QUESTION? YOU SAID YOUR PARTNER WAS SHOT BY MOSES TANENBAUM.
DOES THAT MEAN IT WAS *YOU* WHO KILLED TANENBAUM, *THE IMPERIAL GANGSTA?*
ONE SHOT. POOOFFF!
IT WAS AN HONOUR THING.
THE DEATH OF HOLY MOSES WAS IN ALL THE NEWSVIRTS FOR *WEEKS*. I CAN'T BELIEVE I ACTUALLY KISSED THE GUY WHO DID IT.
REALITY CHECK, SENORA.
JUST TO BE SURE.
¡AY! HIT THE ASPHALT. SENORA BROADWAY! I CAN'T WRESTLE TONGUES WHILE SOME WAZZER IS SHOOTING AT US!
BLAM! BLAM!

I GOT YOU NOW. YOU PUKING GROT-BAGS!
COME HERE AND SAY THAT!
BRAAAAAAPPPP!

OPEN WIDE AND SAY "AHHHHHHHH".
BAMM!
BAMM!
BAMMM!
BAMMM!

COME ON. KAISER WON'T BE FAR BEHIND.
YOU GOT A TRAIN TO CATCH...

FLUGE EISENBAHN
INTERCONTINENTAL MONORAIL TERMINUS
THERE'S A NON-STOP HYPER TO ISTANBUL IN ABOUT SEVEN MINUTES.
IT'LL TAKE ME OUT OF PYE'S JURISDICTION.

GO BUY YOUR TICKET, SENORA. ONE WAY.
I'LL KEEP WATCH IN CASE KAISER SHOWS.

YOU WANNA TELL ME WHAT'S GOIN' ON, RETARD?

SINISTER! YOU'RE MEANT TO BE RESTING! THAT BULLET WOUND WON'T NEVER HEAL IF YOU DON'T TAKE IT EASY.
OH WELL I'D LOVE TA BE CONVALESCING, SO I WOULD, BUT I GETS THIS CALL FROM PORKY PIE, NO LESS, ASKIN' ME TA GO REIN IN ME CRAZY PARTNER!

SEEMS YOU'VE RUN OFF WITH SOME BIRD OF HIS!
SHE WAS IN TROUBLE. IT WAS MY NIGHT OFF. I'M ALLOWED.

SHE'S PLAYED YOU FOR A SUCKER, DEX. SHE WANTS OUT OF THE BUSINESS, SO SHE EMPTIED PORKY'S CHECKING ACCOUNT AND RAN.
SHE JUST COOKED UP SOME SOB-STORY TA GET YE T'WORK FER NUTHIN'.

WELL? DEX? AIN'T YE GONNA SAY ANYTHIN?
WAIT FOR ME HERE. I GOTTA TRAIN TO SEE OFF.

ATTENTION! THE OH-SIX HUNDRED ISTANBUL NON-STOP IS PREPARING TO LEAVE FROM PLATFORM NINE! ALL PASSENGERS PLEASE BOARD NOW!

TIME FOR YOUR BIG FAREWELL SCENE, SPIT-SWAPPERS!

YIIIIIIG-G-G-G!
BA-BOOOOMM!

LOOK LIVELY, BUD, OR THE LADY MIGHT MISS HER TRAIN.

SO LONG, SPORT! IT'S BEEN WILD!
HAVE A NICE LIFE, MELODY BROADWAY.
WHAT WILL YOU TELL PORKY?
A LIE, I SHOULD THINK.
COME ON. YE MAY'VE LOST THE GIRL, BUT BREAKFAST IS ON ME...

NEXT PROG **WISH UPON A CZAR!**

SINISTER DEXTER

WISH UPON A CZAR

Script: Dan Abnett

Art: Simon ("S.B.") Davis

Letters: Steve Potter

Originally published in *2000 AD* Progs 992 - 993

SINISTER DEXTER

WISH UPON A C2AR — PART 1

AND THIS IS DOWNLODE, THE CITY THAT TAKES ITS SHOTS. NEAT.

IT'S THE STROKE OF TWELVE, CENTRAL EUROPE TIME, AND DOWN IN THE CHINAGATE DISTRICT, THINGS ARE REALLY COOKING...

BOOM!!! BLAM! BLAM! BBAM! BLAM!

"SO WHAT IS THIS ABOUT, FOR GOD'S SAKE?"

"AS I HEARD IT, NOODLE SAM'S OUTFIT WANNA SEW UP THE LAUNDRY CONCESSION IN THE GARMENT DISTRICT, AND THE ABADDON CHAPTER BOYS ARE DISPUTIN' THE RIGHT."

"¡VAYASE! SINCE WHEN HAVE THE CHAPTER BEEN INTERESTED IN CLEANLINESS?"

"HEY! IT'S JEST WHAT I HEARD, OKAY? PASS THE DIM SUM."

I TELL YOU, AMIGO, IT'S GETTING TO BE THERE ISN'T A QUIET CORNER *TO* THIS TOWN.

LET ME HEAR YOU SAY *"GANG WAR"*, BUDDY.

SCRIPT DAN ABNETT
ART S.B. DAVIS
LETTERS STEVE POTTER

WHOOMMFF!
WOW.
WHAT?
PHOSPHOR-FRAG. LOOKS LIKE THE CHAPTER'S JUST WON THAT LAUNDRY CONTRACT.
THESE DIM SUM ARE *GREAT*, AREN'T THEY?
FOUR COURSES AND A BANANA FRITTER LATER...
...Y'SEE, PAL, WHAT I'M TALKIN' ABOUT IS *ATTRITION*. ALL THE RIVAL OUTFITS, A-SLAMIN' AND A-HUSTLIN', ALL WEARIN' AGAINST EACH OTHER, TRYIN' TO MAKE IT TO THE *NUMERO UNO* SPOT...
...NO ONE WILL COME TO ANY GOOD FROM IT, I TELL YE.
TIS LIKE A *CIVIL WAR*. 'TWILL BE THE *RUINATION* O' THIS FAIR CITY!
EVERY CHEAP HOOD AND MOB-BRAT FIXIN' TO FILL THE SHOES O' HOLY MOSES NOW HE'S DEAD.
GUESS WE SHOULDN'T HAVE KILLED HIM THEN.

EYES UP, FINNIGAN! WE GOT SOME COMPANY!
SAFETIES OFF, DEXY-BOY! THAT'S VANYA — THE CZAR'S MAIN MAN!
PRIVYET, BOYS! LONK TIME NO SEE!
YEAH, YEAH! PRIVYET YERSELF, VANYA... HOW'S IT HANGIN' MATE?
WE WILL START CUTTINK THE KRAP, BOYS. THE CZAR WANTS TO SEE YOU. SO BE GETTINK IN DE KAR.
OH YEAH?! GIMME ONE GOOD REASON?!
RACHIIK! SHUNK-SHUNK! CHA-CHAKK! RIIK
GOOD REASON...

SHORTLY, AT MISHKA'S BATH HOUSE ON HUNTERWASSER...
MR SINISTER! MR DEXTER! KAK PAZHIVAYETI, MY FRIENDS?

WE'RE DOIN' FINE, BIG GUY. REAL DANDY IN FACT.
'CEPT THAT AN HOUR AGO YER TRAINED BABOONS WAVE GUNS IN OUR FACES. MESELF, I'D KINDA LIKE TA KNOW WHAT THIS IS CONCERNING.
BUT OF COURSE YOU WOULD! AND I WOULD HAVE COME TO YOU TO DISCUSS IT IF IT HADN'T BEEN BATHTIME.
I'LL BE DIRECT. THE GANGWAR MUST BE SETTLED, QUICKLY AND CLEANLY.
LEMME GUESS. YER GONNA HIRE US TO KILL ALL YER RIVALS?
QUITE THE REVERSE, MR SINISTER. I'M HIRING YOU TO KEEP THEM ALL ALIVE.

"GENTLEMEN, THIS IS MY PLAN. I HAVE INVITED ALL MY RIVAL CRIMELORDS TO ATTEND A SUMMIT WHERE WE MAY TALK THROUGH OUR DIFFERENCES LIKE CIVILISED BEINGS.
"I HAVE CHOSEN A SECLUDED AND NEUTRAL LOCATION OUTSIDE THE CITY. AND I WANT YOU TWO TO PROVIDE THE SECURITY FOR THE EVENT.
"YOU ARE THE ULTIMATE NEUTRALS. YOU ARE THE ONLY GUNHANDS IN THE CITY THAT EVERYONE TRUSTS."
THE MEKROPOLIS, CITY LIMITS, TWO DAYS LATER...
THIS PLACE BRINGS BACK MEMORIES. BOY.
ME AND SWEET CAITLIN O'ROURKE IN THE BACKSEAT OF A RUSTIN' TANK.
PLACE GIVES ME THE SHIVERS. ALL THIS DEAD METAL.
FER SHAME, RAMONE! THIS IS SCRAPYARD HEAVEN! THE MOTHER OF ALL JUNKHEAPS!
THE FACT-TOTEM'S PROXIMITY DETECTOR JUST TRIPPED. OUR GUESTS ARE ARRIVING.
WHATEVER. LOOK SHARP.
G-BLEEB!
FIRST UP, IRISH STU AND HIS MERRY BOYS. CONTRABAND AND PROTECTION ARE THEIR TWIN FORTES.
RRRRRRRRRRRRRRRR
TOP OF THE MORNING, FINNIGAN.
PUNCTUAL AS EVER, STU.
PORKY PYE. INFO-BROKER EXTRAORDINAIRE. HE RUNS A DATA EMPIRE THAT STRETCHES FROM HAMBURG TO HYDRABAD.
ENOUGH OF THIS FARCING ABOUT, OKAY? LET'S DO BUSINESS.

WHEN WE'RE ALL HERE, MR PYE.
YOU'RE DEXTER, AREN'T YOU? THE GUN SHARK?
WE MEET AT LAST.
THAT BUSINESS WITH MELODY BROADWAY*. YOU GONNA MAKE MORE OF IT?
ANCIENT HISTORY, MR DEXTER. JUST BE SURE NOT TO CROSS ME AGAIN.
*see PROG 990-1
NEXT, THE SAWN-OFF SHOGUN, DIAMYO OF THE POST-YAKUZA CULT-GANGS. A DEMON-GOD OF DESIGNER NARCOTICS, SHIFTED THROUGH HIS VIRCADE OUTLETS.
THE SHOGUN EXPRESSES HIS CORDIAL GREETINGS.
BULLY HALLIDAY AND HER CELL-BLOCK H FEMINIST MOVEMENT. RUNS A MULTI-BILLION D-BILL ENTERPRISE FOUNDED ON PROSTITUION, GAMBLING AND HARDCORE VIRTS.
OKAY, YOU JERKS. DON'T WASTE MY TIME.
...AND THE CZAR HIMSELF, HEAD OF DOWNLODE'S RUSSIAN MAFIA.
FRIENDS. GOOD TO SEE YOU ALL.
LET'S TALK TURKEY.
MATE, DIS IS EITHER GONNA GO REAL SWELL OR REAL BAD. ALL THE CRIME HEADS OF DOWNLODE GATHERED IN ONE PLACE...
RECIPE FOR DISASTER, FINNIGAN. WHAT ARE THE CHANCES THAT NONE OF THEM WILL TRY FOR THE HIT OF THE CENTURY.
AND THEN GUESS WHO'S GONNA BE SMACK IN THE FIRING LINE..?
NEXT PROG GREATEST HITS!

SINISTER DEXTER
WISH UPON A CZAR PART 2
AND THIS IS DOWNLODE, THE CITY THAT NEVER GOT THE BREAKS IT DESERVED.
IT'S HIGH NOON, CENTRAL EUROPE TIME, AND OUT BEYOND THE CITY LIMITS, IN THE JUNKSCAPE OF THE MEKROPOLIS, THE FUTURE HANGS IN THE BALANCE...
THE CZAR, MOBLORD OF THE RUSSIAN MAFIA, HAS CONVENED A MEETING OF HIS RIVALS IN AN ATTEMPT TO END THE BRUTAL GANGWAR THAT HAS SPLIT DOWNLODE.
AND WHAT BETTER PLACE FOR PRIVACY AND NEUTRALITY THAN THE CITY'S SCRAP GRAVEYARD?
AND EVERYONE'S HERE, LORDS OF THE UNDERWORLD, PRINCES OF DARKNESS ALL...
SCRIPT DAN ABNETT
ART S.B. DAVIS
LETTERS STEVE POTTER
IRISH STU OF THE EMERALD EARLS...
NO WAY AM I GIVIN' UP THE DOCKS! I'M ALREADY SIXTY GRAND IN THE HOLE THANKS TO BACK HANDERS...
THE UBER-YAKUZA BOSS KNOWN AS THE SAWN-OFF SHOGUN...
(humourous retort) BAD BUSINESS ETHICS. I THINK YOU MUST (ironic overtone) EDUCATE THRU PUNISHMENT.
BULLY HALLIDAY OF THE SOUTHSIDE FEMS.
WHO CARES WHAT YOU THINK, MOTOR-MOUTH?
THE INFO-BROKER PORKY PYE...
THIS FROM A WOMAN WHO WAS THROWN OUT OF CZECHOSLOVAKIA FOR TALKING TOO LOUDLY.
...AND THE CZAR HIMSELF.
LET'S KEEP TO THE POINT, MY FRIENDS.
BY THE TIME WE LEAVE HERE TONIGHT, I WANT TO HAVE THE CITY OPERATIONS CARVED UP BETWEEN US IN A WAY THAT IS MUTUALLY AGREEABLE. NONE OF US CAN AFFORD THE GANGWAR ANY LONGER.
THANKS TO THEIR REP FOR BEING THE MOST IMPARTIAL GUN SHARKS IN THE CITY, SINISTER AND DEXTER HAVE LANDED THE JOB OF KEEPING THE PEACE AT THE SUMMIT.
IT'S GONNA GET BLOODY, DEX. YOU MARK ME WORDS.
AFORE THE DAY'S OUT, WE'RE GONNA LAND UP IN THE MIDDLE OF SOME SERIOUS DO-DO.

MAYBE SO, MAYBE NO. WE DO OUR JOB AND WE COULD COME OUT OF THIS LOOKING *VERY* SHARP. *PLUS,* WE'LL BE WELL IN WITH WHOEVER GETS THE TOP JOB.
BZZZKT!
DEXTER TO REX. YOU SEE ANYTHING WE SHOULD BE WORRIED ABOUT, AMIGO?
THE SHARKS HAVE BROUGHT THEIR TRUSTY NARK – "NERVOUS" REX MONDAY – TO MAN THE MAKESHIFT EARLY WARNING POST.
SNRRFFGG! NOT SO FAR, MR DEXTER. ACTUALLY, IT'S VERY DRAFTY UP HERE. I'M GETTING A CHILL ON MY KIDNEYS.
AND I SHOULDN'T BE HERE ANYWAY. I'M ALLERGIC TO RUST.
¡AY VAYASE! DEXTER OUT.
HOW'S NERVOUS? DON'T TELL ME... NERVOUS AS EVER?
C'MON. LET'S SWING ROUND THE PERIMETER AWHILE.
I SAY WE SHOULD *ALL* GET A CUT OF THE NARCOTICS ACTION!
(curt and abusive oath). NOT ACCEPTABLE.
JESUS! STUNTY AIN'T GONNA GIVE ON *ANYTHING* IS HE?
CHECKING YOUR WATCH *AGAIN* MR PYE?
IT'S A NEW WATCH. I LIKE LOOKING AT IT.
DO GO ON. I THINK IT WAS THE CZAR'S TURN TO INSULT SOMEONE.

Ahrm... T-THIS IS REX TO DEXTER. MY SCANNER'S JUST REGISTERED TWO NEW CONTACTS MOVING INTO THE AREA.
FINNIGAN AND I WILL SPLIT UP AND SCOPE 'EM OUT. DIRECT US TO 'EM...
...O-OKAY. THERE'S ONE C-COMING IN FROM THE SOUTHWEST ZONE.
WELL I NEVER...
...IT'S THE ABADDON BIKER CHAPTER.
OH PUKE! WE'RE RUMBLED!
GREASE THAT IRISH SMUGFUNT!
YOU GUYS FIGURE TO MOVE UP OUTTA LITTLE LEAGUE BY SMOKING THE BIG TIMERS, HUH?
I THINK NOT, YOU DOZY HOGS!
RAMONE? I JUST STOPPED A BUNCH O' CHOPPER-CHUMPS FROM SPOILIN' THE CZAR'S PARTY. HOW'S THINGS YOUR END?
I'M ON TOP OF THE OTHER CONTACT RIGHT NOW, AMIGO...

OKAY, WISEASS, THAT'S F-
LITTLE PIG, LITTLE PIG, LET ME COME IN...
...OH PUKE! FINNIGAN! IT'S A KILLDROID! SOME CRAZY'S SICKED A KILLDROID ON US!
STAY BACK. YE HEAR ME, DEX? ME AN' ME HEFTY FIREPOWER WILL BE RIGHT WID YE!
NEGATIVE, MR SINISTER! HOLD YOUR POSITION! MR DEXTER WILL HAVE TO MANAGE ALONE!
I'VE JUST STARTED TO TRACK A THIRD CONTACT COMING IN THROUGH THE LANDFILL ABOUT SIXTY METRES TO YOUR LEFT!
ALL RIGHT, DAMMIT! I'M ON IT! TELL DEX TO WATCH HIMSELF!
THIS IS ALMOST FUN.
REX? IT'S FINNIGAN! I'VE FOUND THAT THIRD CONTACT. IT'S A PACK O' BULLY HALLIDAY'S GIRL GUIDES!
COO-EE! LADIES! TIME FER YER MAKEOVER!
BRAPPP
HOLY JULIE! GUT THE GUN SHARK BEFORE HE DOES US!

CHOOM! CHOOM!
FANK! FANK! FANK!
Hmmm... AN AWFUL LOT OF SHOOTING GOING ON OUT THERE.
YOU HIRED THOSE TWO-BIT GUN SHARKS FOR SECURITY, DIDN'T YOU, CZAR? I HOPE THEY'RE UP TO THE JOB.
THEY'RE BOTH PROBABLY DEAD ALREADY. TIS TIME I TOLD YE WHAT WUZ COMIN' DOWN.
I HIRED THE ENTIRE ABADDON CHAPTER. THEY'RE RIDING IN FER YER BLOOD, BOYS AN' GIRLS. IN A FEW MOMENTS, THEY'LL BE HERE, AND ME SUPREMACY WILL BE ASSURED.
(negative exclamation). LOW PROBABILITY OF YOUR (robust perjorative) HIRED THUGS PREVENTING (including sense of physical opposition) MY KILLDROID FROM (colourful execution euphemism) ALL OF YOU.
YOU HAVE (small quantity) MINUTES OF LIFE LEFT.
GET REAL. AN ANDROID? MY JILLS ARE MOVING IN RIGHT NOW.
FACE IT, STUMPY... I'M GONNA BE QUEEN BEE AROUND HERE.
TAP
SO YOU ALL DOUBLE-CROSSED EACH OTHER, HUH? GOOD. I ANTICIPATED SUCH AN EVENTUALITY.
MY NET PROGRAMS WILL HAVE STRIPPED YOUR PERSONAL DATA FILES AND BANK ACCOUNTS BY THE TIME ANY OF YOUR KILLERS GET HERE. INFORMATION LIKE THAT IS LIFE OR DEATH. IF YOU WANT TO MAKE IT THE FORMER, YOU'LL SUBMIT TO ME...
I GAVE YOU ALL CHANCE. A CHANCE TO TALK AND WORK THINGS THROUGH.
INSTEAD, YOU PLOT AND MACHINATE TO KILL EACH OTHER AND TAKE THE DOWNLODE CROWN YOURSELVES. I AM JUST GLAD I AM NOT ABOVE SUCH TREACHERY...

...WHICH IS WHY I SENT THIS SIMULACRON IN MY PLACE. THERE'S A CLOSE-FOCUS NUKE IN ITS CHEST CAVITY.

IT'S A TEN SECOND FUSE.

NOW I DON'T THINK WE'VE COME OUTTA THIS LOOKING VERY SHARP AT *ALL*, DO YOU?

THAT'S TRUE ENOUGH. EVERYONE'S BEEN NUKED. TO ME, THAT DON'T SAY "SUCCESSFUL DAY'S WORK".

MR DEXTER? MR SINISTER? I'M GETTING A MESSAGE FROM THE CZAR...

HE SAYS "T-THANKS FOR THE WORK, YOU REALLY MADE THE DEAL LOOK CONVINCING." HE'LL SEE YOU AT THE BATH-HOUSE TO ARRANGE PAYMENT.

WELL *DAMN!* THE SUCKER'S STILL *ALIVE!* GUESS THAT MEANS HE'S *TOP DOG* NOW.

THOUGH HE MIGHT'VE *WARNED* US HE WUZ GONNA PULL A STROKE LIKE THAT.

STILL... GOTTA ADMIRE A GUY WHO BRINGS A *NUKE* TO A GUNFIGHT.

NEXT PROG FAMILY MAN!

FAMILY MAN

Script: Dan Abnett

Art: Henry Flint

Letters: Steve Potter

Originally published in *2000 AD* Prog 994

AND THIS IS DOWNLODE, THE CITY THAT FELL AND COULDN'T GET UP.
IT'S EARLY-TO-BED, CENTRAL EUROPE TIME, AND IN FRED QUIMBY MEMORIAL PARK, FINNIGAN SINISTER DECIDES NOT TO MENTION HIS PARTNER'S NEW HAIR COLOUR. INSTEAD HE SAYS--
SINISTER DEXTER
FAMILY MAN
SO WHAT'S AN ACCOUNTANT WANT WITH A PAIR O' WOUNDMAKERS LIKE US?
SCRIPT DAN ABNETT
ART HENRY FLINT
LETTERS STEVE POTTER
GUESS WE'LL FIND OUT SOON ENOUGH. BUT GET THIS – HE'S CALLED DUNCAN DONAT. CAN YOU BELIEVE THAT STOOPID NAME?
OH SURE! SHAME HE DON'T HAVE A SENSIBLE MONICKER LIKE YE, RAMONE ALGONQUIN WINNEBAGO DEXTER!
NOW YOU KNOW I GET TOUCHY ABOUT THAT!
ALRIGHT ALREADY! I WUZ JEST RAGGIN' ON YE.
ICE CREAM
I THINK I SEE OUR MAN UP AHEAD. AND CHECK OUT THE MR SUGARFIX AT YOUR EIGHT O'CLOCK.
SUGERFIX
TWO BULLET-MONKEYS WITH NINE MIL BULGES IN THEIR PANTS, TRYING TO LOOK ANYWHERES BUT AT US.

MR DONAT? MR DUNCAN DONAT?
ARE YOU THE GUN SHARKS I HIRED?
I'M DEXTER, THIS IS MY ASSOCIATE SINISTER.
TOP O' TH MORNIN' TO YE, MR DONAT!
WE'LL BE TAKING A BRISK LITTLE WALK NOW, SENOR.
OH PUKE! THEY AIN'T BACKING OFF!
OKAY RAMONE, ME OL' MUCKER – DO YER MAGIC THANG!
KLA-CHK!
KLA-CHK!
FILL YOUR HANDS OR FILL YOUR PANTS. CHOICE IS YOURS.
TAKE IT EASY, BUD.
WE DON'T WANT THAT KINDA TROUBLE.
WELL, THAT WAS PAINLESS. DIDN'T EVEN HAVE TO KILL 'EM.
SO, THOSE GUYS FROM SOME OUT OF TOWN OUTFIT OR SOMETHING?
"THOSE GUYS", MR DEXTER, WERE FROM THE DEPARTMENT OF TAXATION.

Cafe
SO, MR DONAT - WHY DOES AN ACCOUNTANT NEED OUR PROTECTION?
LARGELY BECAUSE I WISH TO REMAIN ALIVE, MR SINISTER. FOR THE LAST TWO YEARS, I HAVE BEEN THE CHIEF FISCAL ADVISOR TO A MR BRONSKY HAMMER.
"BALLPEEN" HAMMER? THE MOB BARON?
I DON'T ASK WHAT HE DOES, MR DEXTER. I JUST DO HIS BOOKS.
UNFORTUNATELY, HIS CAREER HAS ATTRACTED THE UNWELCOME ATTENTION OF THE TAXMAN AND THAT HAS PLACED ME IN SOMETHING OF A PREDICAMENT.
THIS AFTERNOON, I HAVE TO HAND OVER MR HAMMER'S YEAR END ACCOUNTS AT A RENDEZVOUS HERE IN FRED QUIMBY. I'M CERTAIN BOTH THE IRS AND EXCISE WILL ATTEMPT TO STOP THAT.
I HAVE THEREFORE TAKEN THE PRE-EMPTIVE MEASURE OF HIRING YOU BOTH TO EXPEDITE THE HAND OVER, AS PER REVENUE BOARD REGULATION 28F.
HEH! HOW ABOUT THAT! I'VE NEVER BEEN A LEGITIMATE BUSINESS EXPENSE BEFORE!
UMM, MR SINISTER? NINE AND ONE HALF PERCENT IS NOT AN ADEQUATE GRATUITY. AND YOU MAY WANT TO RETAIN THE BILL FOR YOUR EXPENSES CLAIMS.
NOW I THINK OF IT, DID YOU GET A RECEIPT FOR THE ICE CREAM YOU WERE SUCKING WHEN WE MET? SUCH JOB-RELATED SNACKS CAN ALWAYS BE CLAIMED UNDER SUNDRIES.
OBOY! IT'S GONNA BE A LONG AFTERNOON.
YEAH, BUT IT WON'T KILL US.

...BLAH BLAH WHICH MEANS AN OVERALL DEDUCTION AS PER THE NET YIELD OF THE CLAIM PORTION SPREAD OVER TWO FISCAL YEARS...
YE CAN THINK ABOUT ENTERIN' YER GOB UNDER THE "SHUTTIN' UP" COLUMN ABOUT NOW, DONAT. WE'RE ALMOST AT THE DROP.
TOLD YE THIS WHOLE GIG WOULD BE SWEET N' NEAT, DEXY BOY.
WHAT'S THE WORD, BOYS?
THE WORD IS TAX-FRAUD.
HAND OVER THE BOOKS OR WE SLAMDUNK DONAT.
DEPT OF TAXATION
BLAM
BLAM
BLAM!
BLAM
YOU DON'T SAY!
DEXY! WE BIN SPRUNG!
¡VAYASE! THERE ARE GUN-GOONS COMING OUT OF THE SHRUBBERY! IS THIS REALLY YOUR IDEA OF "EASY MONEY" YOU IDIOT!?
I TAKE IT ALL BACK! C'MON, DONAT! MOVE YER PUKIN' YING-YANG OR WE'RE GRUYERE!
BAM!
BAM!
POW!

FINNIGAN! I'M OUT!
KLIK! KLIK!
S'OKAY. RAMONE ME BOY! I'M TAGGED AN' IN THE RING!
CHOOM!
CHOOM!
CHOOM!
CH-CHOOOM!
I DON'T WANT TO DIE! I'M UNDER-INSURED!
MAKE FER THE BAND-STAND!
JUMPIN' JONAH! I NEVER THOUGHT I'D BE RUNNIN' FOR ME LIFE FROM A GANG O' TAX-JOHNNIES!
PAK!
WHIZZ!
CHOOM!
WALK IN THE PARK, YOU SAID!
FOR GOD'S SAKE! WILL YOU TWO STOP BICKERING AND START EARNING YOUR FEE BY PROTECTING ME?!?
CHOOM!
TAKK!
PANG!
HEY! THIS IS OUR COVER!
PUKE OFF – WE WUZ HERE FIRST!
RED
RED
RED

HONK IT ELSEWHERE, BARFGARGLE!
WAIT! THERE'S NO NEED FOR COLOURFUL IDIOMS, MR SINISTER!
CHAKK!
PING!
THESE ARE THE MEN MR HAMMER SENT TO MEET WITH ME.
THEY ARE? SO WHAT'RE YE DOIN' IN HERE, GIRLS? WHY WEREN'T YE AT THE DROP LIKE ARRANGED?
WE'RE IN HERE 'CAUSE THANKS TO YOU, THIS PARK HAS TURNED INTO A COMBAT ZONE.
THE TAX OFFICE GOT SO SPOOKED THAT YOU WERE MINDING DONAT, THEY SENT IN A WHOLE ARMY TO COLLAR HIM!
WE'RE ALL DEAD, MAN! DEAD!
NO TAX-GEEK'S GONNA KILL ME. WHADDYESAY, DEX?
I'M WITH YOU, MAN. BUT MR DONAT MIGHT FIND HIMSELF CHARGED A LITTLE EXTRA FOR THE BLOCK BOOKING.
FINE! FINE! I'LL EVEN PAY YOUR AMMO AND FUNERIAL FEES. JUST DO SOME-THING!
OKAY, TAX-DWEEBS- LET'S SEE WHAT YOU'VE GOT!
From "Yankster's Guide to the Sights of Downlode": "...following the infamous "Audit Showdown" of '66, Fred Quimby Municipal was closed for extensive restoration and re-planting work. The memorial tomb of the Unknown Excise Man was opened in '73, displaying a brass funeral urn made out of the quarter million spent shell cases recovered from the park."
"It is said that the echo of gunfire still rolls around the lake on long winter afternoons. Admission 2 eurorubles, last admittance dusk, closed Wednesdays."
THE END

LEARNING KURV

Script: Dan Abnett

Art: David Millgate

Letters: Steve Potter

Originally published in *2000 AD* Prog 1023

LEARNING KURV
BLOCKB
S·F·X
FLICKS
AND THIS IS DOWNLODE, THE CITY THAT COULDN'T ESCAPE IF IT WANTED TO.
SCRIPT DAN ABNETT
ART DAVID MILLGATE
LETTERS STEVE POTTER

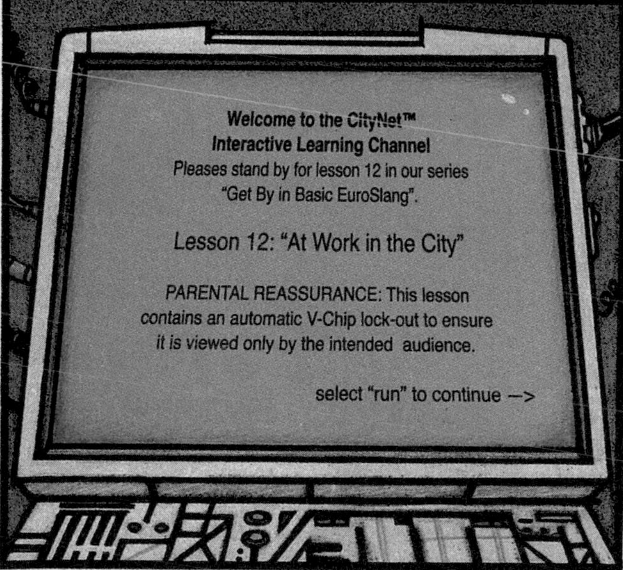
Welcome to the CityNet™
Interactive Learning Channel
Pleases stand by for lesson 12 in our series
"Get By in Basic EuroSlang".
Lesson 12: "At Work in the City"
PARENTAL REASSURANCE: This lesson contains an automatic V-Chip lock-out to ensure it is viewed only by the intended audience.
select "run" to continue –>

Background data commences:
The Vircade District of Downlode is famous for its nightlife. Look at all these people! They've come to sample the fun on offer in the Virtual Arcades and the Game-O-Ramas! Lucky them, eh?
Of course, a visitor wouldn't get far without a good working knowledge of EuroSlang. This lesson has been designed to cover basic words and phrases pertinent to this location.
LUCKY NITE
GREENBACK JACKS!
POPCORN

Lesson begins. Listen and repeat
SEE THE MAN
SEE HIM RUN
RUN MAN RUN
OY!
PUKEHOLE!
SKINS
ALE
WOTCHIT!

SEE THE MEN
SEE THEM RUN
RUN MEN RUN
BAD NEWS!
GUN SHARKS!
WHOOOA!

SEE SINISTER
SEE DEXTER
SEE THE MEN RUN
MARCHETTI! YA PUKIN' FLECK O' HORSE FLOP! RUNNIN' WON'T SAVE YA!
¡VAYASE! HE SURE IS FAST!
Difficult words:
"Horse Flop" - see Lesson 43 "At The Macrobiology Seminar"

SEE THE MAN
SEE THE CAB
WATCH OUT MAN
Oh puke! Oh puke! Oh puke!
VROOOM!
TAXI
De NIRO
Useful words:
CAB BRAKES SUDDEN

SEE THE MAN FLY UP
HEAR HIM GRUNT
GRUNT MAN GRUNT
gnnuff!
WHNNFFF!

• YOU! YOU • • • OF A NO-GOOD •! • YOUR • • WITH A RUSTY • •!
oohhh...
NB: Soundtrack has been edited for family viewing.

GET BACK! GET AWAY FROM ME YOU PUKERS!
SEE THE GUN
POW SAYS THE GUN
POW POW POW
BAM!
BAM!
BLAMM!

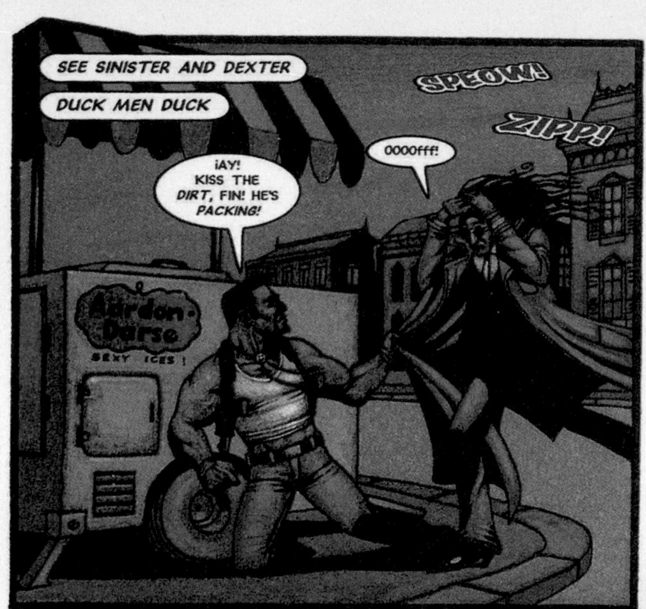
SEE SINISTER AND DEXTER
DUCK MEN DUCK
SPEOW!
ZIPP!
¡AY! KISS THE DIRT, FIN! HE'S PACKING!
OOOOfff!
Aardon-Darse
SEXY ICES!

THANKS THERE, DEX. MARCHETTI NEARLY POPPED ME GOOD.
HEY... ANYTIME, AMIGO.
SEE THE MEN
HEAR THEIR MACHO TALK
BOND MEN BOND

HE'S RABBITING!
C'MON! I AIN'T GONNA LET THIS LITTLE GOB-STAIN GET AWAY!
SMELL THE FEAR
PEOPLE ARE FRIGHTENED
STAY DOWN PEOPLE
Useful words:
INVOLUNTARY STAIN INSURANCE DRY-CLEANERS

LOOK
THE MEN RUN AGAIN
THE MEN RUN INTO THE ALLEY

THE ALLEY IS DARK
Useful words:
DEAD-END TRAPPED RATHOLE
MILLGATE

Ohh, puking heck! Save me!
SEE THE LADDER
FIRE LADDER
SAFETY LADDER
MARCHETTI! COME DOWN, Y'FOOL! WHY DELAY THE INEVITABLE?
• YOU • • • YOU RODE IN ON!
SEE THEM ALL
SEE THEM CLIMB
CLIMB HIGH MEN

SEE THE WINDOW
SEE THE LIGHT
TAKE THE CHANCE

SORRY MISS! JUST PASSIN' THRU!
AEEEEEEIIIIEEEE!
SEE THE GIRL
HEAR HER SCREAM
Useful words: CHARGES OFFENSE PERVERT

HERE COME MEN
RUN MEN RUN
SCREAM GIRL SCREAM
AAEEEEEIIIIEEEE!
PARDON US, I'M SURE, SWEETCHEEKS!
Useful words:
INTRUDER DECIBEL FRACAS CUTEY HOOTERS

DON'T I KNOW YOU FROM SOMEWHERE, DARLIN? THAT BIRTHMARK ON YER HIP IS AWFUL FAMILIAR...
THERE AIN'T NO TIME FOR THAT NOW, YOU EEEEJIOT!
YANK!
Useful words:
LECH DROOL INCORRIGIBLE TROUSERS

THERE HE IS!
OH •!
SEE THE MAN
NOWHERE TO RUN
NOWHERE TO HIDE

SEE THE MAN
SEE HIM DRAW
SLICK DRAW MAN
OKAY, YOU • PUKEHOLES! LET'S DO THIS! LET'S DO THIS!

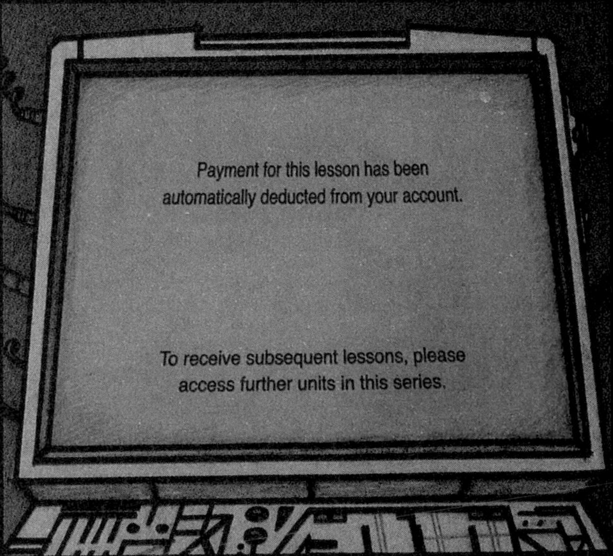

NEXT PROG: GUNSHARK VACATION!

GUNSHARK VACATION

Script: Dan Abnett

Art: Simon ("S.B.") Davis

Letters: Steve Potter

Originally published in *2000 AD* Progs 1024 - 1031

SINISTER DEXTER
GUNSHARK VACATION PART 1
THE NIGHT IT ALL BEGINS IS JUST LIKE ANY OTHER IN ASBESTOPOL, VACATION CAPITAL OF THE BLACK SEA'S SUNSHINE COAST.
IT'S JUNE, LATE, HOT... THERE'S BUSTLE ON THE STREETS. LIQUORED-UP RATINGS FROM THE NAVY YARD ON FURLOUGH. BOARDROOM YAHOOS FROM DOWNLODE IN TOWN FOR THE WEEKEND.
EVER SINCE ODESSA GOT NUKED IN THE BORSHCH WARS OF '52, ASBESTOPOL'S BEEN THE RESORT OF CHOICE FOR CENTRAL EUROPE'S JETSETNIKS AND PARTY-BEASTS ALIKE.
SCRIPT DAN ABNETT
ART S.B. DAVIS
LETTERS STEVE POTTER
ZHELEZNAYA BABA WATCHES OVER IT ALL. THE 'STEEL WENCH', RELIC OF THE LOST SOVIET ERA WHEN THE TOWN'S ECONOMY DEPENDED ON SMELTING, NOT SUNBLOCK.
NOWADAYS, SHE'S A NOVELTY KEY-FOB, A SOUVENIR PAPER-WEIGHT AND A WHOLE SUB-GENRE OF DIRTY JOKES.
BUT THIS IS THE PLACE WE'RE INTERESTED IN. THE BAWDWALK, ON THE OLD SREDNY PIER OFF THE MARINA FRONT.
THIS IS WHERE IT ALL STARTS, IN THE MOST NOTORIOUS GO-GO PALACE ON THE BLACK SEA, ONE HOT NIGHT IN JUNE...
THE BAWDWALK
BIG GIRLS!
MUSCLE BABES
DANCIN'
ALL NUDEY!

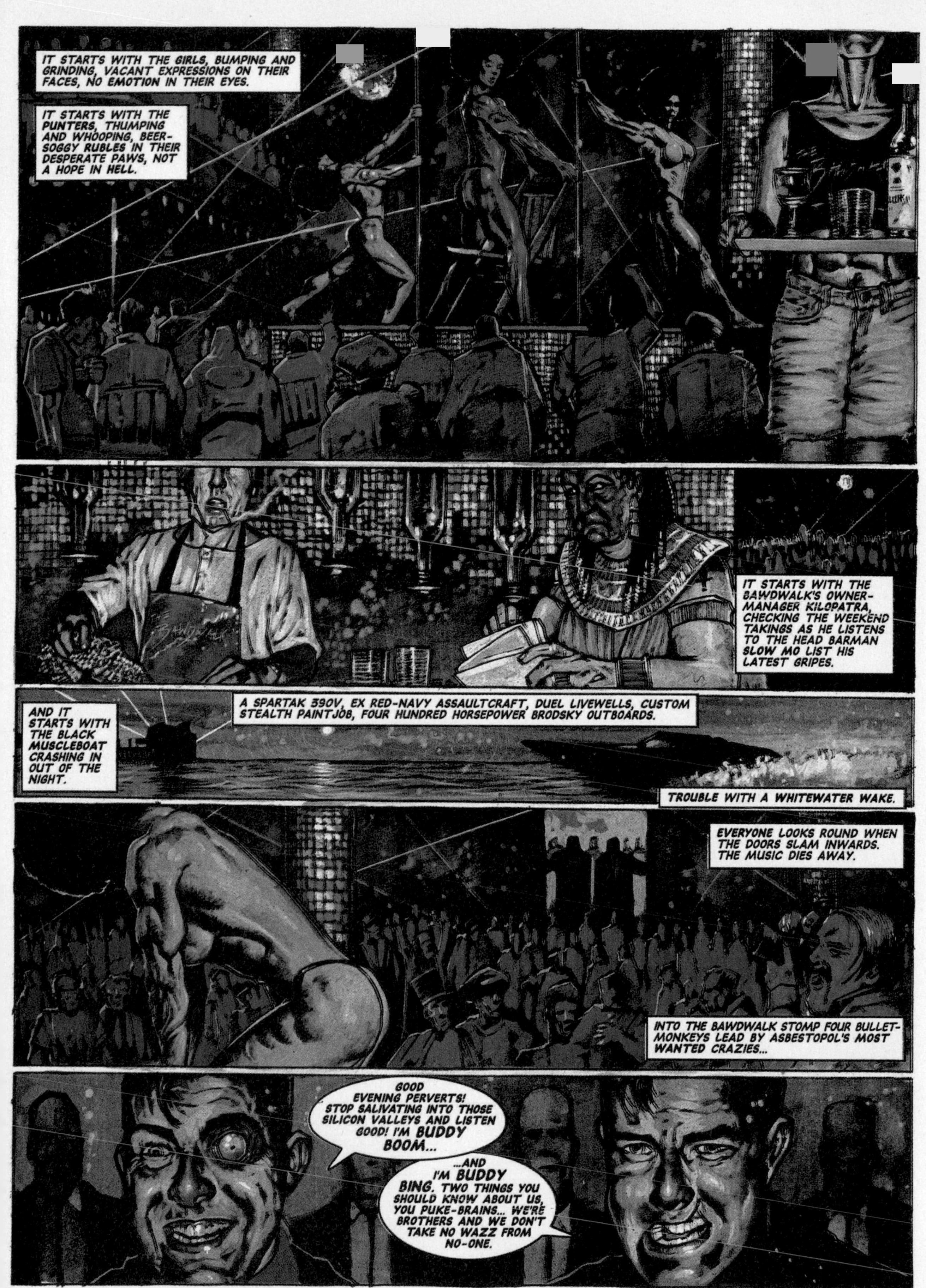
IT STARTS WITH THE GIRLS, BUMPING AND GRINDING, VACANT EXPRESSIONS ON THEIR FACES, NO EMOTION IN THEIR EYES.
IT STARTS WITH THE PUNTERS, THUMPING AND WHOOPING, BEER-SOGGY RUBLES IN THEIR DESPERATE PAWS, NOT A HOPE IN HELL.
IT STARTS WITH THE BAWDWALK'S OWNER-MANAGER KILOPATRA, CHECKING THE WEEKEND TAKINGS AS HE LISTENS TO THE HEAD BARMAN SLOW MO LIST HIS LATEST GRIPES.
AND IT STARTS WITH THE BLACK MUSCLEBOAT CRASHING IN OUT OF THE NIGHT.
A SPARTAK 390V, EX RED-NAVY ASSAULTCRAFT, DUEL LIVEWELLS, CUSTOM STEALTH PAINTJOB, FOUR HUNDRED HORSEPOWER BRODSKY OUTBOARDS.
TROUBLE WITH A WHITEWATER WAKE.
EVERYONE LOOKS ROUND WHEN THE DOORS SLAM INWARDS. THE MUSIC DIES AWAY.
INTO THE BAWDWALK STOMP FOUR BULLET-MONKEYS LEAD BY ASBESTOPOL'S MOST WANTED CRAZIES...
GOOD EVENING PERVERTS! STOP SALIVATING INTO THOSE SILICON VALLEYS AND LISTEN GOOD! I'M BUDDY BOOM...
...AND I'M BUDDY BING. TWO THINGS YOU SHOULD KNOW ABOUT US, YOU PUKE-BRAINS... WE'RE BROTHERS AND WE DON'T TAKE NO WAZZ FROM NO-ONE.

WHAT THE HELL DO YOU SCUZZPUCKS MEAN BY BURSTING IN HERE LIKE THIS? I PAY YOUR BOSS OFF REGULAR, RAIN OR SHINE.
NEWSFLASH, QUEENIE. THE PRICE JUST WENT UP.
MR O'FISCH WANTS ANOTHER GRAND EACH WEEK.
THAT'LL DESTROY MY BUSINESS!!
WAKE UP AND SMELL THE FLOWERS, FAT BOY...
...PAY THE MONEY. YOU DON'T WANT TO KNOW ABOUT THE ALTERNATIVE.
WELL, I DO.
WHO THE PUKE SAID THAT?
SHOW YOURSELF!
I SAID... I FER ONE'D LIKE TA KNOW WHAT YE HAVE IN MIND. ARE YE GONNA KILL FOLK? BLOW THE JOINT UP?
Y'SEE, I'M JUST A TOURIST MESELF, AND I'VE FLAT RUN OUT O' CASH TA STUFF IN THE G-STRINGS OF THESE LOVELY YOUNG LADIES...

...SO I WUZ KINDA HOPIN' FOR SOME *ENTERTAIN-MENT*.
AND YOU *SCUZZPUCKS* ARE *THE* MOST *ENTERTAININ'* THING I'VE SIN *ALL WEEK*.

YOU AIN'T NO *TOURIST*. THAT *DOWNLODE* ACCENT O' YOURS...
...YOU'RE SOME *CITY-MUSCLE*, AIN'T YOU?
I'M A *TOURIST*, SO I AM! LOOK I'LL *PROVE* IT...

I GOT *EVERYTHIN'* YER TOURIST BRINGS ALONG.
FACTOR *70* SUNBLOCK.

DICK RANCID
A TRASHY *BONKBUSTER* FROM THE AIRPORT.

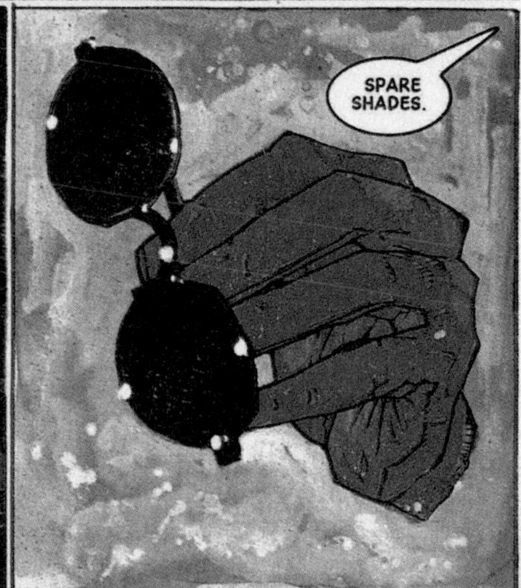

SPARE SHADES.

AND A FULLY AUTO, UNDER-AND-OVER, READ-'EM-AN'-WEEP, H-'N'-K SCATTAMATIC MINIGUN.

NEXT PROG: PHISH SUPPER!

SINISTER DEXTER
GUNSHARK VACATION 2
Greetings from Azbestopol-on-Black Sea
Dear Rex,
Our vacation down on the Black Sea Riviera has started off pretty good. We are already making lotsa friends, like Kilopatra, a guy who runs an ace and classy go-go club called The Bawdwalk. We ain't even had to whack no one yet. Please remember to feed my goldfish. See you in a few weeks.
Your pal
Ramone Dexter
P.S. Sinister says "Hi".
"Nervous" Rex Monday,
appt. 234,
Gogol Platz,
Downlode
YOU GUYS SAY YOU'RE LOOKING FOR WORK? LET'S GO TALK ABOUT THAT.
HEY, SLOW MO! BRING A ROUND OF PEPPER VODKAS TO MY OFFICE.
SURE THING, KILOPATRA.
COME IN! ME CASA SU CASA.
MA-MA! WILL YE LOOK AT ALL THIS-
SCRIPT DAN ABNETT
ART S.B. DAVIS
LETTERS STEVE POTTER
SONY
-COOL STUFF.
WORDS OUTTA ME MOUTH, PAL. "WILL YE LOOK AT ALL THIS COOL STUFF" IS PRECISELY WHAT I WUZ ABOUT TO SAY.
GLAD YOU LIKE IT.
POUR THE SMILEY JUICE, MO.

SO– WHAT BRINGS A PAIR OF BIG CITY BODYCOUNTERS TO THE VACATION CAPITAL OF HADES?
WE NEED TO LAY LOW FOR A WHILE UNTIL SOME DUST SETTLES IN DOWNLODE.

BIG DUST?

LET'S JEST SAY WE WUZ WALKIN' IN A PARK ONE DAY.

A PARK? FRED QUIMBY? YOU BOYS PULLED THE FRED QUIMBY BLOODBATH?

AMONG OTHERS. SO YOU SEE SENOR KILOPATRA, WE HAVE TO KEEP OUR HEADS DOWN FOR A SPACE.
WE WERE OWED A FAVOUR BY THE CZAR OF THE RUSSIAN MOB. HE SUGGESTED WE CAME DOWN HERE AND LOOKED YOU UP.

THE CZAR?! WHY DIDN'T YOU SAY STRAIGHT OFF? HE AND I GO WAY BACK. USED TO RUN A TASTY LITTLE FAKE-MINK RACKET OUT OF THE CRIMEA BEFORE THE ECO-BACKLASH.
I'M HAPPY TO GIVE SANCTUARY TO ANY FRIENDS OF THE CZAR'S!

AND O' COURSE, IN RETURN, WE'LL ACT AS UNOFFICIAL MINDERS FOR YER ESTABLISHMENT. SORT OUT ANY PROBLEMS YE MIGHT HAVE.

LIKE FER STARTERS... THOSE GOONS WE SCARED OFF. WHO WUZ THEY WORKIN' FOR?
LET ME TELL YOU ABOUT THEIR BOSS...

"PHILLY O'FISCH IS THE LOCAL MOB-KING. CONTROLS NINETY PERCENT OF THE ACTION IN EVERY RESORT FROM HERE TO THE DANUBE.
"THE BAWDWALK IS PART OF THE MISSING TEN PERCENT. I HAVE TO PAY HIM PROTECTION OF COURSE, BUT WHAT HE REALLY WANTS IS TO ADD MY CLUB TO HIS EMPIRE.
"SO HE SENDS HIS BOYS ROUND EVERY NOW AND THEN TO PUT THE FRIGHTENERS ON ME AND MY GIRLS."
"WELL NOW, I FIGURE ME AN' ME PARTNER SHOULD PAY THIS MR O'FISCH A VISIT TOMORROW. WHERE CAN WE FIND HIM?"
"FANTASY ISLAND, OUT IN THE BAY."
AHOY THE SHORE! WE'RE HERE TO SPEAK WITH MR O'FISCH!
I GOT NUTHIN' TA SAY TA YOU. SLING YER HOOKS.
AND NO FUNNY BIZ LIKE YOU PULLED LAST NIGHT.
YEAH, WE'RE READY FOR YOU THIS TIME.
IF THAT'S THE WAY YE WANT IT, LADS.
LET'S GET IT OVER WITH.

BUDDY BOOM. .44 CALIBRE MAZZ LONGSLIDE. REACTION TIME POINT SIX OF A SECOND. TWO SHOTS, NO HITS.
BUDDY BING. "SKARAB" MACHINE PISTOL. REACTION TIME POINT EIGHT OF A SECOND. THIRTY SEVEN SHOTS. NO HITS.
FINNIGAN SINISTER. HANDS IN POCKETS. REACTION TIME NOT APPLICABLE. NO SHOTS. NO HITS.
RAMONE DEXTER. TWIN RUGER CUSTOM NINES. REACTION TIME UNRECORDABLE. TWO SHOTS. TWO HITS.

NEXT PROG: WATERWORLD [OF DEATH]!

SINISTER DEXTER

GUNSHARK VACATION PART 3

Greetings from Azbestopol-on-Black Sea

Dear Rex-y-boy,
Me and Ramone are havin' a blinder of a vacation down here on the Black Sea. Landed us a job working as muscle for a local go-go club run by a guy called Kilopatra. Had a fracas on the first day with the local moblord, name of Philly O'Fisch. But that's all behind us, and today we're escort for some richnik tourists.
Best regards
Finnigan Sinister
P.S. Feed Dexter's goldfish, okay?

"Nervous" Rex Monday,
appt.234,
Gogol Platz,
Downlode

GOOGOL BAY, TEN MILES OUT FROM THE RESORT TOWN OF ASSBESTOPOL. BEST BLUEFIN GROUNDS IN THE BLACK SEA, SO THEY SAY.

THIS IS THE FLYING FELUCCA, A STATE-OF-THE-ART GAME-CATCHER BELONGING TO THE BAWDWALK CLUB, AND HIRED FOR THE DAY BY A WEALTHY PATRON.

MAXIM BURKHARD, SLEAZE-MOGUL, PORN-PRINCE. TODAY HE FANCIES DOING A WHOLE HEMINGWAY RIFF AND KILLING A BIG FISH.

THAT'S FRANZINE.
SHE'S ALONG FOR THE RIDE. ANY RIDE, SO LONG AS IT'S FREE. SHE'S ONLY SLEEPING WITH BURKHARD BECAUSE SHE THINKS IT'LL FURTHER HER CAREER.

STOOPID BROAD. YOU'RE SCARING THE FISH.
A CHARTER LIKE THIS NEEDS ONE OTHER VITAL COMPONENT...
SCRIPT DAN ABNETT
ART S.B. DAVIS
LETTERS STEVE POTTER

...FISHING GUIDES.
SO I WUZ MEANIN' TA ASK YE, DEX... ACCEPTING O' COURSE THIS IS THE CUSHIEST GIG WE EVER PULLED...
...DO YE KNOW THE FIRST PUKIN' THING ABOUT FISHIN'?
AND DO YE WANT ANOTHER TINNIE, BY THE BY?
SONY
GRACIAS.
AMIGO, THE CHANCES OF ACTUALLY CATCHING ANYTHING ARE LOW TO NON-EXISTENT.
SO OUR BASIC IGNORANCE NEED NEVER COME TO LIGHT, OKAY?
SOUND PLAN.
GOOD OF OL' KILOPATRA TO SET US UP WITH THIS WORK. GETS US OUTSIDE, WE SEE A LITTLE SUN... AND A WHOLE LOT OF FRANZINE.
YEAH...
VAYASE! LIFE IS SO SWEET MY TEETH ARE WORRIED.
THREE MILES AWAY AS THE SPRAT SHIMMIES...
...BIG FISH, BIG FISH, THIS IS SMALL POND, OVER. DO YOU READ?

BIG FISH HERE. IS THAT YOU, ANDROPOV?
HOOKHAND ANDROPOV AT YOUR SERVICE, SIR! I'M IN POSITION AS AGREED. ALL I NEED NOW IS CONFIRMATION YOU'VE PUT THE FUNDS IN MY ACCOUNT.

CHECK IT YOURSELF. IT'S ALL THERE.
SO I SEE. YOU'RE A GENTLEMAN, SIR.
WELL, I'LL GET TO WORK THEN.

WEAPON DEDICATED AND RELEASED
I UNDERSTAND IT'S AN OLD WARTIME MODEL YOU'RE USING?
THE VERY BEST, SIR. RED NAVY SURPLUS. THEY DON'T MAKE 'EM LIKE THIS ANY MORE.

"THESE BABIES DON'T STOP FOR NUTHING!"
TICK
TICK
TOCK
TICK
TOCK
TOCK
TOCK

TARGET ACQUIRED
THOSE DOWNLODE PUKES WILL BE OUT OF YOUR HAIR BY LUNCHTIME.

MISTER ANDROPOV, THAT'S JUST WHAT I WANTED TO HEAR.

...BUT YE KNOW WHAT I *REALLY* MISS? THE CHEESE STEAKS AT LONELY DONEGANS.

AY! MAN, I HEAR *THAT!* ASBESTOPOL'S GOT SOME GOOD EATERIES, BUT *NOTHING* BEATS THE HOME COOKING AT LONELY'S!

EEK!

LIKE THE...THE *CHORIZO SLICES,* Y'KNOW? THAT TANGY, SPICY, TONGUE-HUMPING FLAVOUR...

STOP, STOP! YER KILLIN' ME!

SAY...

...WHERE'D THE BABE GO?

NEXT PROG: BITE ME!

SINISTER DEXTER

GUNSHARK VACATION PART 4

Greetings from Asbestopol-on-Black Sea

Dear Rex,
Sinister and I are maxing out on sun down here on the Black Sea. We're spending most nights working as bouncers for a go-go club in Asbestopol, a joint run by a cool guy called Kilopatra. Our day job is as fishing guides, taking rich pukes out into the bay.
Felicidades!
Ramone Dexter
P.S. Hey, you will feed my goldfish, won't you?

"Nervous" Rex Monday,
appt. 234,
Gogol Platz,
Downlode

HERE'S THE DOPE. IN GOGOL BAY, SINISTER AND DEXTER HAVE DISAGREED WITH SOMETHING THAT'S TRYING TO EAT THEM...

DEXTER! TIME TO LEAVE, ME LADDIO!

SCRIPT DAN ABNETT
ART S.B. DAVIS
LETTERS STEVE POTTER

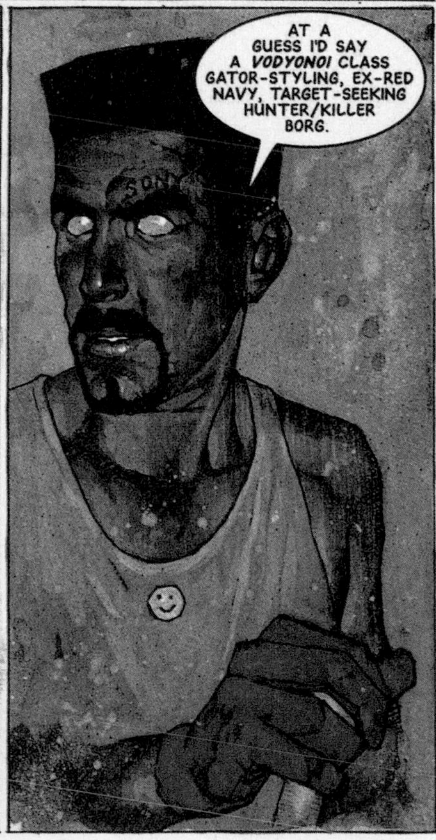

COULD YOU BE LESS SPECIFIC?!
CYBER-DEATH ON FOUR STUMPY LEGS.
THANKS.
MAXIM BURKHARD, PORN-PRINCE, RICH PUKE...
...AND ANY MINUTE NOW, GATOR-BAIT.
IT'S GOING RIGHT UNDER US!
DID YOU TWO BRAIN-DONERS HEAR ME? I SAID--
AAAAAAGGH!
WHHHMMMMACHH!
HOLY MOLEY! IT'S DEADLY AT BOTH ENDS!
FISH ME OUT YOU STUPID PUKES!
FISH ME OUT!
WHHOOOOOOMCHHHHHKKKK!

THIS IS REAL BAD.
REAL, REAL BAD.
TELL ME ABOUT IT! NO WAY ARE WE GETTING A TIP NOW!
ACCORDING TO THE FISH SONAR IT'S SIX FATHOMS BENEATH US, PROBABLY DIGESTING BURKHARD.
THE CREEP WHO'S OPERATING IT MUST BE NEARBY.
AND GUESS WHAT? THE SCOPE'S PAINTING A BOAT JUST TWO KLICKS AWAY.
C'MON!
MR O'FISCH? THOUGHT YOU'D LIKE TO KNOW YOU INVESTED WISELY IN MY SERVICES.
MY GATOR JUST ENGAGED THOSE TWO GUN-MONKEYS FROM DOWNLODE.
I'LL HAVE TO CALL YOU BACK – I HEAR BOAT ENGINES.
HOLY PUKE! IT'S THEM!

TOP OF THE MORNIN'! WOULD YOU BE TRYIN' TA KILL AT ALL?
CAUSE IF YE ARE COULD YE LAY OFF?

HA HA HA! I CAN'T SHUT IT DOWN!
THAT'S THE BEAUTY OF THE VODYANOI MODEL! IT'LL KEEP GOING TIL IT GETS YOU!
EVEN IF I COULD ABORT IT, I WOULDN'T! HOOKHAND ANDROPOV DOESN'T LISTEN TO DESPERATE MEN!

HOOKHAND ANDROPOV SOUNDS LIKE A STOOPID GUY, THEN.
ME PAL'S RIGHT THERE. ME MINIGUN FAIR WON'T MAKE A DENT ON YER CYBER-GATOR...

...BUT I THINK IT'LL BLOW THE KNACKERS OUTTA YER TUB!
CHOOM!
CHOOM!

KTHOOM!

Y-YOU THINK YOU'VE WON, DON'T YOU?

WELL, THINK AGAIN! YOU'VE JUST SLOWED THE GATOR DOWN! THE CONTROL FEEDBACK WILL SELF-REPAIR!
SOONER OR LATER, ONE DAY, IT'LL *FIND* YOU AGAIN!

HE'S RIGHT. THE IVANS REALLY *BUILT* THOSE THINGS. ONE DAY...
HEY, PAL! THAT'S *ONE* DAY.
TODAY, WE LIVE.

HEY? YOU JUST GONNA LEAVE ME HERE?

THIS TALE HAS TWO EPILOGUES...
IN ONE, A CYBORG GATOR LOCKS IN FUGUE MODE AS ITS FRAZZLED BRAIN SLOWLY RECONFIGURES ITS MURDEROUS INEXORABLE MISSION...

IN THE OTHER, A NEW ACT WALKS INTO THE BAWDWALK. THESE DAYS, SHE CALLS HERSELF BIKINI ATOLLS, SINGER, DANCER AND PARTY-TIME GODDESS.

I'M LOOKING FOR KILOPATRA. HE HERE?
BUT SHE USED TO BE DEMI OCTAVO. NEXT TO HER, A HELL-BENT SOVIET KILL-BORG IS THE LEAST OF SINISTER AND DEXTER'S PROBLEMS...

NEXT PROG: DEMI MONDO!

SCRIPT
DAN ABNETT
ART
S.B. DAVIS
LETTERS
STEVE POTTER
Greetings from Azbestopol-on-Black Sea
Yo, Rexy!
Me an' Ramone's vacation down here at Azbestopol is going great. We're workin' at a go-go club called the Bawdwalk. There's a new act startin' tonight, by the name o' Bikini Atolls. Word is, she's hotter than a blast furnace!
Yer Budster,
Finnigan Sinister
P.S. Sorry ta harp on, but remember ta feed Dexter's goldfish, y'hear?
"Nervous" Rex Monday,
appt. 234,
Gogol Platz,
Downlode
SINISTER DEXTER
GUNSHARK VACATION PART 5
SO SHE'S HOT, YOU SAY?
RAMONE ME OL' PAL, FROM WHAT I HEAR, "HOT" DOESN'T EVEN BEGIN TA COVER IT.
IT'LL EVEN MAKE PONCIN' UP IN THESE PENGUIN SUITS WORTHWHILE!
WHAT'VE YOU HEARD ABOUT THIS "BIKINI ATOLLS", MO?
SLOW MO, THE BAWDWALK'S HEAD BARMAN...
WHAT I HEARD, SHE'S A HUBBA-WUBBA UBER-MOXIE FROM OFFAWAYS WITH A ZING-ZANG-ZOWIE THAT'LL TAKE YER EYE OUT! YESSIR!
AND THE MAIN POINTS AGAIN IN, LIKE, ENGLISH?
SHHHH! IT'S STARTIN'!
GENTLEMEN! THE NEXT ACT IS NEW TO THE BAWDWALK. BUT SHE COMES WITH IMPECCABLE CREDENTIALS!
MY FRIENDS, THE BAWDWALK PRESENTS...

BIKINI ATOLLS!
Bay-beee! I know that you been stressin' out!
Bay-beee! Why can't you see?! Bay-bee! You're lettin' bad things get on top of you...
Well why not make one of those bad things...
...me?
I TOLD YOU SHE WAS GOOD!
IT'S HER!
VAYASE! IT IS! IT'S–
SHHHHHHH!
–MGLP!

LATER...
NOK! NOK!
BIKINI ATOLLS
IF YOU'RE SOME PERV, GET LOST!
I THINK YE'LL MAKE AN EXCEPTION THIS ONCE, MISS ATOLLS...
...OR SHOULD THAT BE... ...DEMI OCTAVO?
WHAT THE– OH MY GOD!
WHAT ARE YOU PUKES DOING HERE? YOU'LL BLOW MY COVER!
WHICH IS NOT A MILLION MILES AWAY FROM OUR REACTION, MISS OCTAVO.
YEAH, AND IT AIN'T NICE TA CALL THE MEN WHO CAREFULLY SHOT YER HUSBAND NAMES NEITHER.
SO I SUGGEST WE ALL HAVE A WEE GLASS OF HA-HA JUICE AND SEE IF WE CAN'T SORT A WAY OUT OF THIS SITUATION.

ELSEWHERE, AT THE RESORT-PLEX KNOWN AS FANTASY ISLAND...

MR O'FISCH? YOU WANTED TO SEE ME?

PHILLY O'FISCH, THE EMPEROR OF THE BLACK SEA MOBS.

THAT YOU, TONY?

TONY LACUNA, AT YOUR COMMAND, BOSS.

I JUST GOT A CALL TONY, FROM AN OLD FRIEND IN DOWNLODE CITY.

SEEMS THOSE TWO GUN-MONKEYS WHO'VE BEEN CAUSING ME SO MUCH TROUBLE HAVE A HISTORY.

YOU MEAN SINISTER AND DEXTER, PHILLY?

THEY WERE THE ONES WHO DID HOLY MOSES. AND THE WITCH WHO HIRED THEM, MOSES'S SQUEEZE, IS DOWN AT THE BAWDWALK TOO.

THINK OF IT, TONY... THE THREE LOSERS WHO KILLED MY BROTHER MOSES, JUST A BOAT RIDE AWAY.

NEXT PROG: DEXTER'S MIDNIGHT GUNNERS!

SINISTER DEXTER
GUNSHARK VACATION PART 6
Greetings from Azbestopol-on-Black Sea
Me amigo, Rex!
Our holiday plans have been a little spoiled. We have been working as muscle at a go-go club down here on the Black Sea coast. But last night, we found out that Demi Octavo was here too, working under the stage name Bikini Atolls. Now it seems that someone has set the three of us up...
Stay well,
Ramone Dexter
P.S. If I don't make it back, Rex, please remember to keep feeding my goldfish. Gracias!
"Nervous" Rex Monday, appt.234, Gogol Platz, Downlode
EVERYONE IN THE RESORT TOWN OF ASBESTOPOL REMEMBERS THE NIGHT THEY HIT THE BAWDWALK.
TONY LACUNA, THE RIGHT HAND MAN OF MOB-KING PHILLY O'FISCH LED THE BOYS ACROSS THE WATER.
TONY LACUNA WAS THE MADDEST, BADDEST GUN-PLAYER THAT EVER SWUM UP THE DANUBE.
KLIKK!
KLIKK!
THERE WERE PEOPLE IN PARTS OF THE EURO-REPUBLIC HE'D NEVER HEARD OF WHO WERE AFRAID OF HIM.
WHICH PROBABLY EXPLAINS WHY ALL BUT THREE PEOPLE HAD RUN SHRIEKING FROM THE BAWDWALK WHEN THE POWERBOATS ROARED IN.
OKAY, BRING US IN...
SCRIPT DAN ABNETT
ART S.B. DAVIS
LETTERS STEVE POTTER

THE THREE WHO STAYED?

GUN SHARKS SINISTER AND DEXTER PLUS DEMI OCTAVO.

WE'RE GOING TO *DIE*, AREN'T WE?

DEMI, BABY...

WE ARE GOING TA *DIE FIGHTIN'.*
SILLY ME, I THOUGHT IT WAS *BAD NEWS.*

IGNORE MY BUDDY, MISS OCTAVO.
REMEMBER WHAT YOU ONCE CALLED US? "DE BEST GUN SHARKS MONEY COULD BUY".
I STILL BELIEVE THAT, RAMONE...

...BUT I'M ALL OUTTA *CASH*, AND I'M AFRAID WE'RE *ALL OUTTA LUCK.*

DEMI, HONEY... OUR SPECIALITY IS *THE LAST STAND.*
GET YESELF TA COVER, MISS OCTAVO.
TIS ABOUT TA GET *NOISY.*

MOVE IT! NICE AND STEADY!
KRASSSHH!
TONY? THERE'S NO ONE HERE! THEY MUST'VE–
AGHH!
BOOM! BOOM! BOOM!
GYEEGH!
DAMMIT! THESE GUYS ARE SERIOUSLY HEAVY! DON'T GIVE 'EM ANY OPENINGS!
TONY? WE'RE ON THE ROOF NOW.
OKAY, TAKE IT SLOW...
AGGHH!
AKK!
EGGH!
CHOOM! CHOOM! CHOOM!
URHK!

DEXY! THEY'RE COMIN' IN FROM ALL ANGLES!
I JUST PINKED FOUR ON THE ROOF, SO I DID!
BOOM!
BOOM!
CHOOM!
AY VAYASE! THE MAIN BAR'S FULLY BOOKED!
DROP ROUND THE SIDE AND COVER BACKSTAGE!
EIGH!
BOOM!
CHOOM!
GOOD CALL, RAMONE!
A BUNCH O' STAGE DOOR JOHNNIES JUST GOT A PERSONALISED MOMENTO OF THEIR VISIT!
FTOOOM!
AHKK!
GUHHH!
GEEH!
AGHH!
GPUHH!
EIGHH!
HUH? WHAT IN THE NAME O' SAINT JULIE?
BRAKKA BRAKKA BRAKKA BRAKKA!
LAUGH IT UP, IRISH BOY.
YOUR SMART LIP WON'T SAVE YOU NOW.
Ah PUKE.
KILOPATRA' SLO MO!
THOUGHT WE'D LEND A HAND, GUN SHARK.
THIS IS STILL MY CLUB, REMEMBER!

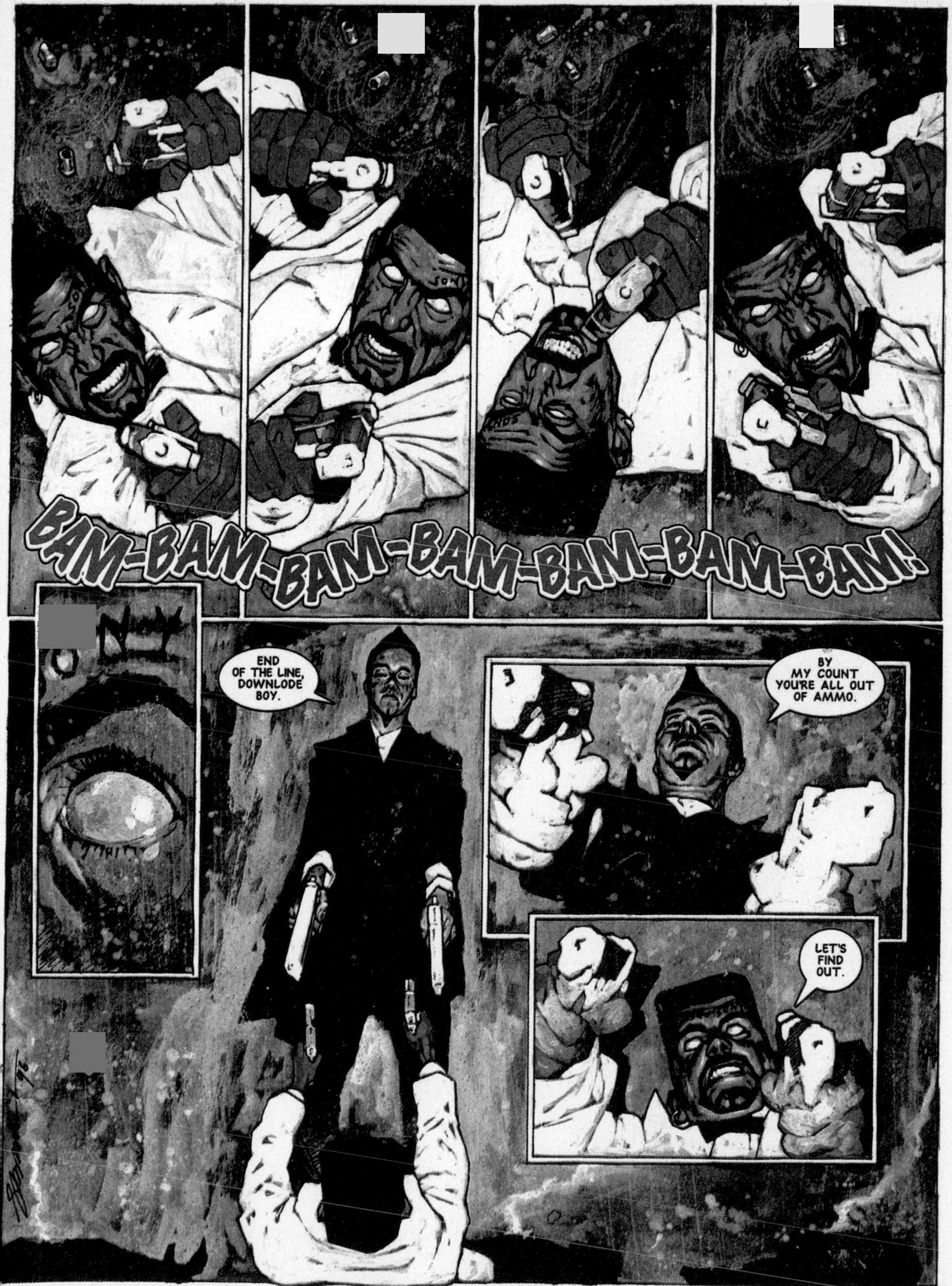

NEXT PROG: THE FINAL ROUND?

SINISTER DEXTER

GUNSHARK VACATION PART 7

SCRIPT DAN ABNETT
ART S.B. DAVIS
LETTERS STEVE POTTER

Greetings from Azbestopol on Black Sea

Rex, Listen up!
As ye knows, we came to the Black Sea resort town o' Asbestopol to lay low. Now we been set up - me and Dex, and ol' Demi Octavo, the ex-squeeze of Holy Moses. The local mob prince, Philly O'Fish, is out to collect for Moses death. We're making our last stand at the Bawdwalk go-go palace. If we don't make it back, ye will remember to feed Dexter's goldfish, will ye not?
Finnigan Sinister
P.S. Ye will! Ye will! Ye will!

"Nervous" Rex Monday,
appt. 234,
Gogol Platz,
Downlode

DOWN AT THE BAWDWALK, IT LOOKS LIKE THE POLIZEI CHALK OUTLINER IS GOING TO BE BUSY TOMORROW.

IN THE BALL ROOM PRIMO ENFORCER, TONY "BLUE" LACUNA PLAYS POSE HARD WITH HALF OF DOWNLODE'S TOUGHEST GUNSHARK DUO...
...RAMONE WINNEBAGO ALGONQUIN DEXTER.
JUST SAY WHEN, LACUNA.

CITY BOY, I GOT YOUR 'WHEN' RIGHT HERE.

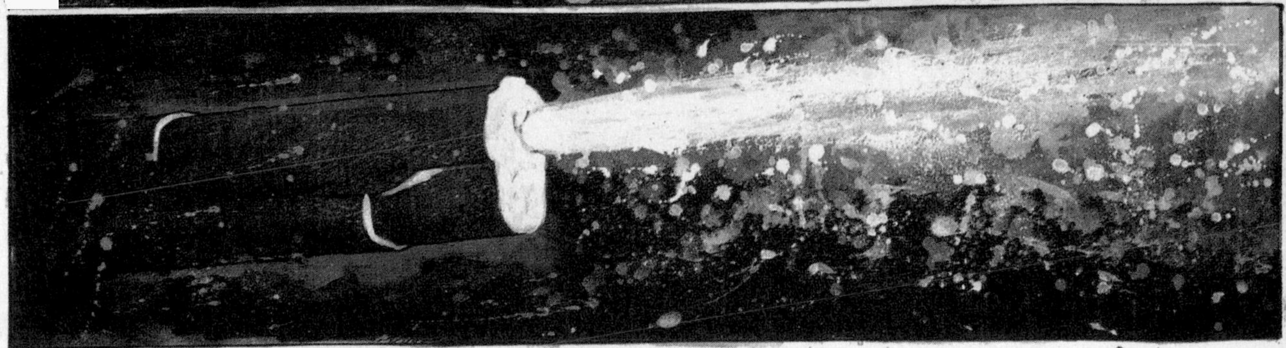

MISS OCTAVO!
DEX. AFTER ALL WE'VE BEEN THROUGH, CALL ME DEMI.
YOU SO SAVED MY LIFE THERE DEMI. I WAS OUT OF LEAD.
THAT'S NOT WHAT I'VE HEARD, RAMONE.
DEX! DEMI! YOU OKAY?
SURE THING, CAMPADRE. MISS OCTAVO JUST GAVE BLUE LACUNA A NEW CENTRAL PARTING.
OH FUDGE! IT'S GOING TO TAKE ME WEEKS TO GET THE BLOOD OUT OF THE TAFFETA!
WHADDYE SAY? QUIT WHILE WE'RE IN FRONT, OR GO FER BROKE?
¡AY VAYASE! ARE YOU KIDDING? O'FISCH JUST TICKED THE "BLOODY VENDETTA" BOX.
HEY! COUNT US IN!
YEAH, I'M ON FOR THE BIG FINISH.
APPRECIATE THE OFFER, GUYS, BUT YOU STAY PUT AND LOOK AFTER MISS OCTAVO...
...FINNIGAN AND ME WILL MAKE SURE O'FISCH GETS HIS CHIPS.

FANTASY ISLAND, RESORT-PLEX HOME OF PHILLY O'FISCH.
IT'S ALL TAKEN CARE OF. I'M EXPECTING MY BOYS BACK ANY TIME NOW.
ONE THING I GOTTA KNOW, CZAR. WHY TIP ME OFF ABOUT THE GUYS WHO SMOKED MOSES?
SINISTER, DEXTER AND DEMI OCTAVO WERE KINGMAKERS, PHILLY.
THEY WERE THE ONLY PEOPLE IN DOWNLODE CAPABLE OF REMOVING MOSES, GIVING ME CONTROL OF THE CITY.
WOULD YOU WANT PEOPLE LIKE THAT ALIVE?
GOOD POINT, LOOK, I HEAR BOAT ENGINES. CATCH YOU LATER.
WHAT THE-

HEADS UP, PHILLY! YER SHARK BAIT, PAL!

KTSMASSSHHH!

NEXT PROG: RETURN TO DOWNLODE?

SINISTER DEXTER
GUNSHARK VACATION
PART 8
AND THIS IS DOWNLODE, THE CITY WHOSE SMILE SEEMS OUT OF PLACE. IT'S MIDNIGHT AND THEN SOME, CENTRAL EUROPE TIME.
THE BULLET TRAIN NOW ARRIVING AT PLATFORM THREE IS FROM ODESSA, DNEPR AND THE BLACK SEA RESORT OF ASBESTOPOL.

WAKE UP, DOWNLODE. THE BOYS ARE BACK IN TOWN.

IT'S TEN MINUTES BY LIFTER TAXI FROM THE RAILHEAD TO PUSHKIN STRASSE, AND THE TOWNHOUSE OF DOWNLODE'S CURRENT MASTER MOBLORD...
SCRIPT DAN ABNETT
ART S.B. DAVIS
LETTERS STEVE POTTER

...CZAR OF THE RUSSIAN MAFIA.

BLAMM! BAM-BAM-BAMM-BAMM!
WHAT IN THE NAME OF-!

WHAT'S GOING ON OUT THERE? VANYA?
VANYA?
T-THERE'S SOMEONE HERE TO SEE YOU, SIR.
FFUMMFF!
EVENIN', CZAR.
DON'T EVEN BOTHER WID THE GUN, SENOR. YOU KNOW HOW FAST WE ARE.
I THOUGHT YOU WERE–
DEAD?
WELL, TO BE SURE, THAT'S HOW YE WANTED IT, WASN'T IT? SENDIN' US OFF ON A NICE VACATION DOWN TO ASBESTOPOL WHERE YER CHUMMY O'FISCH COULD TAKE A POP AT US.
TROUBLE WAS, WE DON'T POP THAT EASY.
FINNEGAN... MY FRIEND... IT WAS NOTHING PERSONAL. IT WAS BUSINESS.
SURE IT WAS. SO'S THIS.
WE WAS TOO DANGEROUS TO HAVE AROUND. WE TOOK OUT THE BIG HOLY ONE, THERE WAS ALWAYS A CHANCE WE'D TAKE YOU.

AND GUESS *WHAT?*
YE WUZ *BANG ON, CHARLIE.* WE'RE PAY-BY-THE-HOUR WOUNDMAKERS, AND OUR METER'S RUNNING.
ONE LAST THING...
W-WHAT?
WE BROUGHT SOMEONE TO SEE YOU.
HIYA, *CZAR.*
SEE MY LITTLE DOGGIE HERE? IT'S AN EX-WARZONE CYBORG MADE TO *KILL* UNTIL MY PALS MESSED WITH ITS PROGRAMMING.
NOW IT DOES *EVERYTHING* I SAY...
SIC THE BAD MAN! SIC 'IM, BOY!

NOOOOOOOOOOOOOOOOOOOOOOOOO!
LATER...
LOOK OUT THERE, YOU PAIR. YOU SEE THAT?
DOWNLODE?
THE FUTURE, RAMONE.
OH. THAT.
THERE'S AN EMPIRE OUT THERE. A KINGDOM OF CRIME, JUST WAITING FOR A NEW SOVEREIGN WITH THE FIREPOWER TO COMPETE.
WHAT DO YOU SAY, BOYS? THE KING IS DEAD.
GOD SAVE THE QUEEN!
I'LL DRINK TO THAT.
WE START MONDAY MORNING, TEN SHARP. AND SINISTER...
...TURN THE SHIRT OFF.
BUT IT'S THE LATEST HOLO-FABRIC C–
OFF!

APPT. 234, GOGOL PLATZ, DOWNLODE, HOME OF "NERVOUS" REX MONDAY.
OH, SO YOU'RE BACK THEN.
GET YOUR HEAD AROUND THIS ONE, AMIGO! DEMI OCTAVO IS THE NEW MOB EMPRESS OF DOWNLODE...
AND GUESS WHO HER NUMERO UNO PISTOLEROS ARE?
JUST IMAGINING GIVES ME AN ACID STOMACH.
STILL CAN'T BELIEVE SHE DIDN'T DIG THE SHIRT. THIS HOLO-WEAVE COST ME A PACKET AT FLOPPY DICK'S-
WILL YOU GIVE IT A REST, ALREADY?
HEY, REX-WE WROTE YOU SOME POSTCARDS.
SORRY, BUT WE KINDA FORGOT TO ACTUALLY POST THEM.
WHY AM I NOT SURPRISED?
SO ANYWAYS... HOW ARE MY GOLDFISH DOING?
WHAT GOLDFISH?
Greetings from
THE END

Prog 1030 Cover by **Simon Davis**

Prog 1024 intro page by **Simon Davis**

Prog 998 Cover by **Calum Alexander Watt**

Prog 981 intro page by **David Millgate**

Dan Abnett is the co-creator of 2000 AD series *Atavar*, *Badlands*, *Sancho Panzer* and *Sinister Dexter*. He has also written *Black Light*, *Downlode Tales*, *Durham Red*, *Flesh*, *Future Shocks*, *Judge Dredd*, *Pulp Sci-Fi*, *Roadkill*, *Rogue Trooper*, *The V.C.s*, *Vector 13* and *Venus Bluegenes*, as well as *The Scarlet Apocrypha* and *Wardog* for the *Megazine*. A prolific creator, Abnett has also written for Marvel, Dark Horse and DC Comics, and he is the author of sixteen novels for the Black Library, including the best-selling *Gaunt's Ghosts* series. His most recent work outside the Galaxy's Greatest Comic is DC's *Legion* and *Superman* and WildStorm's *Mr. Majestic*. Dan Abnett was voted "Best Writer Now" at the 2003 National Comic Awards.

Simon Davis's unique, angular painted style has been a fixture of *Sinister Dexter* for some years now, beginning with his *2000 AD* debut on the series. He has also found the time to create *B.L.A.I.R. 1* and *Black Siddha* as well as contributing to *Downlode Tales*, *Judge Dredd*, *Missionary Man*, *Outlaw*, *Plagues of Necropolis*, *Tales of Telguuth*, *Tharg the Mighty* and *Vector 13*. His most recent non-2000 AD work was on DC's *JLA: Riddle of the Beast*.

Henry Flint is one of the Galaxy's Greatest Comic's rising superstars. Co-creator of *Sancho Panzer* and *Shakara*, his incredibly versatile pencils have also graced *A.B.C. Warriors*, *Judge Dredd/Aliens*, *Bill Savage*, *Deadlock*, *Judge Dredd*, *Rogue Trooper*, *Missionary Man*, *Nemesis the Warlock*, *Nikolai Dante*, *Sinister Dexter*, *Tharg the Mighty*, *The V.C.s*, *Vector 13* and *Venus Bluegenes*. He has even written several *Tharg's Alien Invasions* strips! Flint has also begun to establish himself in American comics, working on anthology titles *AIDS Awareness*, *Ammo Armageddon* and *Monster Massacre*.

Charles Gillespie has contributed to both *2000 AD* and the *Megazine*, illustrating *Sinister Dexter* and *Vector 13* for the former and *Armitage*, *Judge Anderson*, *Judge Dredd*, *The Inspectre* and *Missionary Man* for the latter. He is currently leading the design team for a major forthcoming Xbox video game.

David Millgate is the co-creator of future hit men *Sinister Dexter* and has also illustrated *Brit-Cit Brute*, *Judge Dredd*, *Future Shocks*, *One-Offs* and *Outlaw*. He has recently returned to the *Megazine* to illustrate *Mean Machine*.

Anthony Williams is the co-creator of both *Babe Race 2000* and *Kola Kommandoes*. During his *2000 AD* career he has illustrated *Big Dave*, *Future Shocks*, *Judge Anderson*, *Judge Dredd*, *Mean Arena*, *Mean Machine*, *Robo-Hunter*, *Sinister Dexter*, *Sláine*, *Tharg the Mighty* and, most recently, *The V.C.s*. Williams's work beyond *2000 AD* includes *Batman*, *Fate*, *Green Lantern*, *Superman*, *The Unfunnies* and Games Workshop's *Titan*.